AF593378

Chair

The current state of the art, with the who, the why, and the what of it.

Produced by Peter Bradford
Edited by Barbara Prete

Established 1834
Thomas Y. Crowell
New York

Chair: Copyright © 1978
by Peter Bradford Publishers, Inc.
Published in the United States by
Thomas Y. Crowell, Publishers,
10 East 53rd Street,
New York, New York 10022.
Published simultaneously in Canada
by Fitzhenry & Whiteside Limited,
Toronto.
Library of Congress Catalogue Card
Number 78-60172
ISBN: 0-690-01783-9

Design by Peter Bradford and Wendy Byrne.
Composition by David E. Seham Associates.
Printed by Albert H. Vela.
Manufactured in the United States of
America.

Chair represents the powers, impulses, forces, and motives in a design process. Ultimately it represents the *people* who have them, or exert them. In doing that, it demonstrates that "design" is not an abstract term, it is a very human one.

So is publishing a very human endeavor, strongly effected by the qualities of the people involved. The editors of *Chair* are very grateful for the efforts and cooperation of all participants. In developing the content, Jane Clark and Lisa Taylor at the Cooper-Hewitt and all the lecturers were endlessly cooperative and encouraging, as were all the furniture companies represented.

Especially essential were the contributions of the photographer Michael Pateman, Richard Saul Wurman who reported the AIA competition, and poor Ralph Caplan who never saw the end of us.

In the painstaking process of producing the book, Wendy Byrne (interminably) coordinated, supervised, and prepared art for the project, with the assistance of Anne Todd. Lonnie Browning, Virginia Dajani, Bill Harris, and Wendy Strobel helped research and edit the text and photographs. And the essential qualities of reproduction were supplied by our allies Lloyd Vela, David Seham, Henry Marshall, and their companies.

We are grateful for the perspective of Nicholas Ellison at Thomas Y. Crowell, who believed in and supported the project from its inception. We hope that Nancy Gallt, Mary Chadwick and others in the company know our appreciation.

There is no accurate measure of a professional no matter what his field. And no guide to find the best. In enjoying the superior work of all our contributors, we have simply been extremely fortunate.

Peter Bradford, Barbara Prete

The lecture series "The Evolving Chair", upon which this book is based, was created in late 1976, by the Cooper-Hewitt Museum in New York City.

The Museum, recently designated the Smithsonian's National Museum of Design, provides a unique environment for study in the field of design. Its superb decorative arts and design collection and their various educational programs present the public with a variety of ways in which to explore and understand design. The Museum's collection began in 1897, as the three precocious granddaughters of Peter Cooper, founder of the Cooper Union School, gathered *objets d'art* from around the world and exhibited these openly at the school. Then, through the efforts of its director Lisa Taylor and the Smithsonian Institution, it was moved and made accessible to the public in the renovated Andrew Carnegie Mansion on Fifth Avenue.

Contents

chair (chȃr) n. 1. a seat, especially for one person, usually having four legs for support and a rest for the back and often having rests for the arms. 2. something that serves as a chair or supports like a chair: *The two men clasped hands to make a chair for their lame companion.* . . . 4. a position of authority, as of a judge, professor, etc. 5. the person occupying a seat of office, esp. the chairman of a meeting. . . . v.t. 12. to place or seat in a chair. 13. to install in office or authority. 14. to preside over; act as chairman of. . . . 15. *Brit.* traditionally, to place (a hero or victor) in a chair and carry aloft in triumph . . .—*The Random House Dictionary of the English Language,* Unabridged Edition.

Preface

The function of a chair—an object to sit on—limits its form but does not exhaust the pervasiveness of the chair either as an object or as symbol. From "cathedra" to "chairman," from the throne of God to the humblest hassock, the chair sits large in the popular imagination. A chair can be a sling, a spring, a pedestal—or the sophisticated structures of the Egyptians, the Chippendale workrooms and Bauhaus period. New technology has brought new names, a re-evaluation of human needs, and a new esthetic.

Since most chairs are portable and require minimal storage space, the chair was a favored object of the Hewitt sisters, who opened their study collections in 1897. The Cooper-Hewitt, the Smithsonian Institution's National Museum of Design, houses originals and representations of stages in the evolution of chairs. The development of a Queen Anne chair for example, can be traced through the collections to a reproduction of an earlier Chinese platform with cabriole legs. Additional illustrations depict Baroque influences that raised the base of the platform, added a back, and later arms.

The Doris and Henry Dreyfuss Study Center and the Department of Drawings and Prints offer documentation of chairs dating from the ancient world: antique tombs with chair representations, period rooms from the fifteenth century forward, rare drawings by Pugin and Adam, auction sales catalogues from the 1890s, working drawings of furniture producers before World War I, and color charts on decorating from the 1930s.

In the Decorative Arts Department there are actual chairs from the Italian Renaissance, the early-eighteenth-century Queen Anne chair from the collection of the Earl of Scarsdale, nineteenth-century Belter chairs and sofas, Thonets, papier-mâché side and slipper chairs, Carlo Zen's art nouveau desk chair, and chairs by Josef Hoffmann, Frank Lloyd Wright (from the Imperial Hotel), Breuer, and Eames.

From the Textiles Department there are needlework seats and canvas patterns, Majorelle gilded chairs with silk needlepoint coverings, and swatches going back to Coptic fabric, in all a great resource for contemporary design.

The educational programs at the Cooper-Hewitt combine the resources of the past in its vast collection of 100,000 objects with the contemporary research of distinguished scholars and designers. The Museum's first lecture series on contemporary design was "The Evolving Chair." Notable chair designers and related professionals were invited to explore the what and why of chairs, how they got that way.

Ralph Caplan, design critic and writer, introduced the broad historical, social, and esthetic view of chairs, summarized the discussions, and included a prophecy of chairs-to-be. Associate Dean at the Cooper Union School of Engineering, Mary Blade, discussed the dynamics of shape—chairs as structures characterized according to their mobility and geometry. Ward Bennett, the well-known furniture, interior, and industrial designer, directed his talk to esthetics based on structure, material, and design options. Industrial designer Niels Diffrient brought the participants into an evaluation of comfort versus appearance. Interior designer Joseph D'Urso examined chairs as objects in spatial settings. Nicos Zographos, designer; Donald Gratz, master craftsman; and Charles Stendig, who has introduced so many new designs to America, met on a panel that spanned pure design, the realities of manufacturing, and the possibilities of marketing and distribution.

The meeting of these renowned and diverse professionals as a group was the first effort to coordinate a great collection with the design practice of today for a lay audience. The American Institute of Architects, later sponsored its own competition, a further demonstration of the overall concern for increasing general awareness of the connecting links between scholars, curators, designers, and the rest of us.

The programs of this Museum and the ideas of this book go beyond a situation of chairs.

Jane Clark, Director of Programs
Cooper-Hewitt Museum

In late 1976, the Cooper-Hewitt Museum, sponsored its first lecture program on contemporary design, a series of talks on *The Evolving Chair.* Eight expert practitioners studied the great variety of the chairs' historical, creative, technological and economic contexts. *Chair* presents these perspectives in a manner calculated to preserve their original extraordinary texture of juxtaposed tastes and skills.

Caplan

Ralph Caplan, born in 1925 in Pennsylvania, received his B.A. from Earlham College and his M.A. from Indiana University. He is a writer and communications design consultant, producing publications, exhibition scripts, film scripts, and design and planning services for such clients as *Scientific American,* IBM, Herman Miller Inc., the Smithsonian Institution, UNESCO, and Charles Eames. He was editorial director of the Walker Report on violence during the 1968 Democratic National Convention, and is the former editor-in-chief of *Industrial Design* magazine, and the recipient of many awards for editorial and design excellence. He is a member of the Executive Board of the International Design Conference in Aspen.

There has, to my knowledge, never been a world chair shortage. Yet although the need for still another chair has not yet been established by the Surgeon General, an astonishingly large number of designers go on designing chairs.

When a designer creates a chair that is original in concept, it is enough to make his reputation for a decade. If it is possible to sit in it with anything less than acute pain, this is a bonus.

"Goldilocks sat in the great big chair. It was too hard. She sat in the middle size chair. It was too soft. She sat in the baby chair. It was just right—but it broke when she sat on it."

That is a capsule history of chair design in the Western world. Does it matter? It appears to matter very much. If the world is a stage, then all designers are set designers and the chair is the basic prop.

It is certainly our basic artifact, even though—or because—it has nothing to do with basic survival needs—food, shelter, clothing. The chair is the standard advanced problem for design students and a major challenge for professionals. There has, to my knowledge, never been a world chair shortage. Yet although the need for still another chair has not yet been established by the Surgeon General, an astonishingly large number of designers go on designing chairs. No designer is so maladroit and inept that he cannot make a satisfactory chair; yet few have created chairs that are handsome, sound, comfortable, and healthful. When a designer creates a chair that is original in concept, it is enough to make his reputation for a decade. If it is possible to sit in it with anything less than acute pain, this is a bonus.

Architects in particular find chairs challenging: Mies Van Der Rohe, Eero Saarinen, Marcel Breuer, Le Corbusier, Frank Lloyd Wright, Alvar Aalto—designers search for the right chair solution like biologists hunting for a cancer cure.

They are not alone. A standard exercise in traditional philosophical inquiry has to do with determining whether or not a chair is real. Why a chair? Thoreau lived at Walden Pond in a cabin furnished chiefly with three chairs—one for solitude, two for friendship, three for society.

The chair dominates our language as it dominates our environment. Our ways change, and with them our diction, but whether a group has a chairman or a chairperson, the symbol lingers on. Folksy: Pull up a chair. Formal: Please be seated. Mr. Abercrombie will see you soon.

My father distrusted certain novels and movies because

(Ralph Caplan and his Eames lounge chair) "Why is it so easy for so many kinds of people to have a love affair with this chair?. . . . I have owned one for nearly 20 years, during which I've spent a lot of time admiring it while sitting in a chair that supports me better. But this is far and away my favorite chair. The first time I saw it, in 1956, I knew that I wanted it. I decided to buy one as soon as I deserved it. Realizing at last that I would never deserve it, I got one anyway."—Ralph Caplan, from his lecture "Herman Miller, Adventures in Design", Walker Art Center, Minneapolis, 1976.

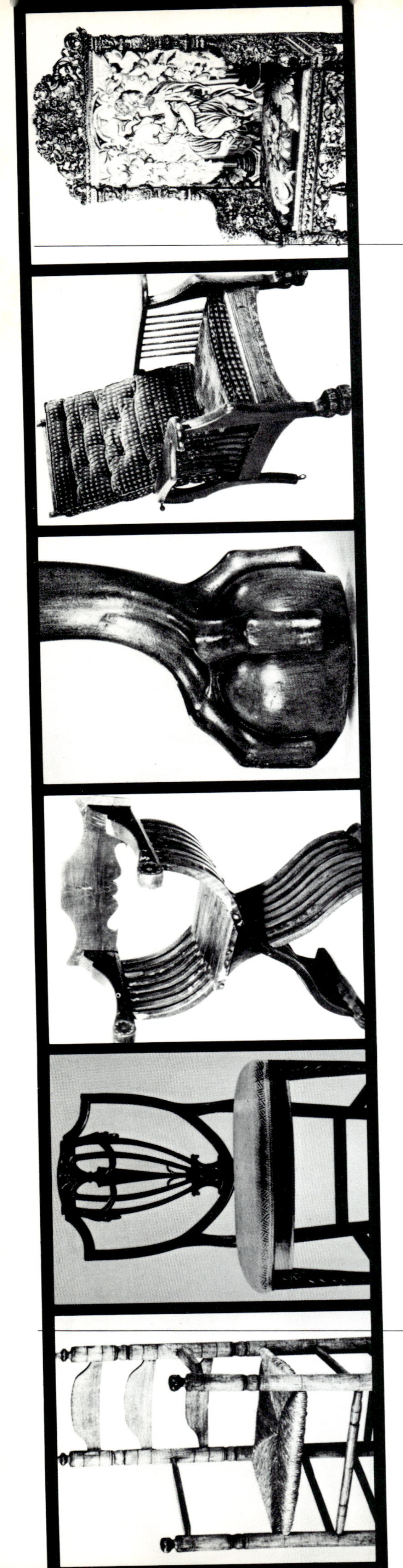

in them people said, "Won't you sit down?" My father didn't believe that people really said that, except in books or movies, and in his experience no one ever did say it. On the other hand, he could have accepted "Sit, sit."

The chair recognizes you, and we recognize the chair. During the Watergate hearings the Department of Justice wondered whether it was legally possible to arrest a sitting President. One of the highest university offices is a chair.

Consider the witness chair, with the witness situated high enough to be displayed to the jury and spectators yet low enough to be intimidated by lawyers. The placement of chairs is one of our oldest forms of gamesmanship. Have you ever had a job interview in which the prospective employer sat *beneath* you?

The role of the chair as an element in human interaction is relatively unstudied. Not to worry. What we need is not research but awareness. You can easily do informal studies of your own. Try taking Polaroid pictures of your living room before and after a party. Many rooms will look quite different. Some will look almost the same, except for peanut shells and glasses and filled ashtrays—it depends a lot on the kind of party giver you are. If the furniture has been radically dislocated, then the usual configuration of your living room furniture is not the same as that for a party. But if the furniture is not out of place, what is the message? That you are always ready for a party? That the furniture is too large to move? That the party was dull, or at least remarkably static? Or that it was a stand-up party?

If it *was* a standup party, it is worth asking why. "No thanks, I'd rather stand" may be a revealing statement. There are social occasions in which guests are afraid to use the chairs, just as Presidential candidates Carter and Ford during their first television debate were afraid to use the Eames bucket seats that forlornly accompanied them. Even during the 27-minute audio failure, neither candidate sat down. To be sure, sitting down would have been a cumbersome process because of the cord running from the throat mikes to the audio equipment. But sitting down is a position of trust, like turning one's back; and these

Chairs are probably more revealing than most objects to those who know how to read them. But design offers clues, not narratives. These chairs can hint at social history, suggesting how much time and skill were available for hand labor. What we can't tell is how these chairs worked as instruments of manipulation, devices designed literally to keep people in their place.

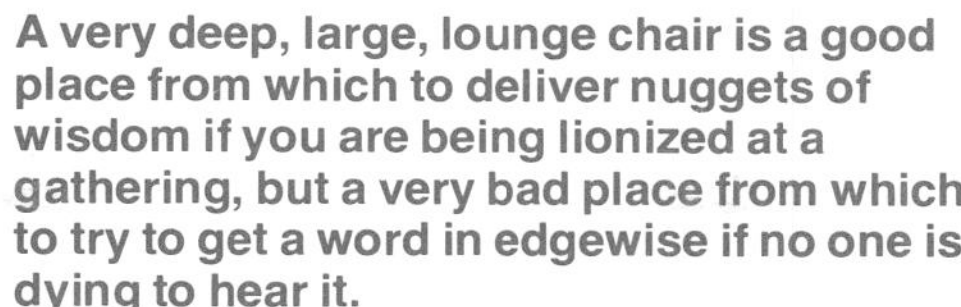

A very deep, large, lounge chair is a good place from which to deliver nuggets of wisdom if you are being lionized at a gathering, but a very bad place from which to try to get a word in edgewise if no one is dying to hear it.

were two men not in a position to trust each other or themselves. If Ford *had* sat down he would have lost the advantage of being taller than Carter. Also, sitting down means having to get up again, risking a fall from gracefulness.

Such concerns, dramatized in a national event that was otherwise devoid of any dramatic interest, affect us all almost every day. Each of us has been in rooms in which some people dominate the conversation not only because of who they are but because of where and how they sit. We have all seen people unable to get into a conversation because of where they managed to place themselves. We have all been in that situation ourselves. A very deep, large, lounge chair is a good place from which to deliver nuggets of wisdom if you are being lionized at a gathering, but a very bad place from which to try to get a word in edgewise if no one is dying to hear it. We have all been stuck in the immediate environment in which we first placed ourselves or in which an obliging hostess has placed us. It is impossible to furnish a room intelligently without taking this kind of thing into account, and that is one reason for the variety of chairs we seem to need.

To some extent, the placement of chairs is not entirely our doing. Products contribute to the design of other products. And products contribute to the design of the spaces in which they are used. Television is a powerful design influence. Until its advent there were very few rooms in which the chairs faced the same way. Chairs used to face other chairs, or a sofa, so that people could talk with or look at one another while they listened to the radio. With television the American living room has been transformed into a convertible theater. And the design of chairs for theater is not the same as the design of chairs for reading.

Which leads us to consider function. Many classic chairs are stubbornly functional. In one of the myriad Bauhaus declarations, Gropius wrote: "In order to create something that functions properly—a container, a chair, a house—its essence has to be explored, for it should serve its purpose to perfection, *i.e.,* it should fulfill its function practically and should be durable, inexpensive, and 'beautiful.'"

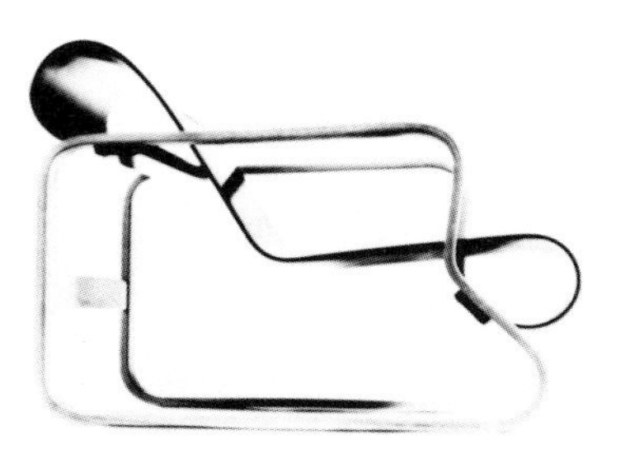

Modern chairs, as used by modern designers for themselves and their modern clients, often amount to a kind of visual name dropping. To wave someone into the right chair is like serving him the right wine. Although this suggests a certain snobbery, it is worth noting that in chair design the appellation "classic" has not only survived, but embraced plastics.

"Life is too short," Parkinson said. "When asked to design a chair, the designer shouldn't sit down and gaze at the sky, saying, 'what is a chair? what are the *elements* of the problem? what is the true philosophy of the problem?. . . .' It all takes too long, and costs too much, and the result is horrible anyway."

As with all counsel of perfection, this one is not especially useful. No one would argue that a chair should not fulfill its function practically, that it should not be durable, or that it should be costly or ugly. But somebody might argue that it is unnecessary to explore the essence every time. At least, somebody *has* argued that—namely, C. Northcote Parkinson, the author of *Parkinson's Law.* "Life is too short," Parkinson said. "When asked to design a chair, the designer shouldn't sit down and gaze at the sky, saying, 'what is a chair? what are the *elements* of the problem? what is the true philosophy of the problem? what is the true philosophy of chairmaking?' It all takes too long, and costs too much, and the result is horrible anyway. Better to agree together on what a chair is. At the end of it, one designer will obviously be better than another."

Parkinson wasn't suggesting that we already know what a chair is all about. He was suggesting that designers don't know but ought to find out, ought to establish some consensus on what a chair means, so that design could proceed as a professional discipline—a professional discipline being one that has some body of knowledge upon which there is qualified agreement.

But the function of a chair is not all that easy to establish. Some years ago a friend of mine praised a chair she owned with the remark, "It is a very good chair for sitting." At the time that seemed a strange feature to single out. Sitting, I thought, is what a chair is *for.* But it isn't, not necessarily. The function of a chair may be to fill a corner, dress up a room, keep a table from looking unattended, organize space, impress people, depress people.

Even when the function of a chair *is* sitting, there is considerable latitude in how that requirement is to be met: a chair may be designed for elegant sitting, for long-term sitting, for brief sitting, for comfortable sitting, for calculatedly uncomfortable sitting, for "seating," which is uncomfortable sitting in large numbers.

Even chairs that are designed primarily for sitting obviously are used for many other things. Exercise. Play. Drying clothing. Storing objects. Making love.

Chair design is humbled by the fact that we *can* sit on almost anything but a cactus plant. Rocks, steps, curbs, packing crates—these all serve very well. If there were no computer designers, we would have to learn to process data with our brains. But if there were no chair designers, none of us would stop sitting down for a minute.

Even when the function of a chair *is* sitting, there is considerable latitude in how that requirement is to be met: a chair may be designed for elegant sitting, for long-term sitting, for brief sitting, for comfortable sitting, for calculatedly uncomfortable sitting, for "seating," which is uncomfortable sitting in large numbers.

Often the true function of a chair is symbolic. If a man's home is his castle, a man's chair is his throne. The gospel according to Archie Bunker is most authoritatively delivered from the nerve center of the household—his easy chair. The director's chair is practical in that it can be easily moved from studio set to location, but that is not its real practicality. The movie industry spends millions of dollars moving heavy equipment around all the time and could haul chairs as easily as it hauls cameras and cranes. The function of the movie director's chair is to carry the name of the director. That's why we all like them, although they can be hell to sit in.

Our most common chair symbols are the so-called modern classics—the Barcelona chair, the "Wassily" and "Cesca" chairs, the Eames leather lounge chair. But the most deeply symbolic chairs probably are those Goldilocks discovered. And they tell us as much about ergonomics in chair design as most designers know.

The story of Goldilocks and the three bears expresses a close relationship between person and chair: "The moment they stepped into the house they saw that someone had been there. 'Umph!' said the papa bear in his great big voice. 'Someone has been sitting in my chair!' " Notice the indignation and horror: "Someone's been sitting in my chair"—it suggests a kind of rape, an invasion of something highly personal. And notice too that the bear spotted the violation instantly.

Even symbolic chairs have to be sat in, and sitting is itself symbolic. Sitting is not necessarily plopping. It is a movement and can be performed gracefully or brutally. Designers sometimes talk about whether they ought to design for the way people sit or the way people ought to sit, but chair design is usually concentrated on neither, but on how chairs look.

The literature of design is extremely revealing in this regard. There are a fair number of books about chairs. Museum chair collections are described in lavish catalogues. And if you add to these all the commentary on chairs in books that are not about chairs as such, you get

Since chairs historically reflect prevailing art forms, pop art is understandably reflected in contemporary chairs; but novelty chairs confront us with a basic design problem: the absence of constraint. These chairs remind us not to take chairs too seriously, particularly some of these chairs. A 3-dimensional gag is harder to live with even than a repetitive situation comedy.

If a man's home is his castle, a man's chair is his throne. The gospel according to Archie Bunker is most authoritatively delivered from the nerve center of the household—his easy chair. "...'Umph!' said the papa bear in his great big voice. 'Someone has been sitting in my chair!'" It suggests a kind of rape, an invasion of something highly personal.

what amounts to a sizable literature dealing with a single object. Some of our best minds have taken on the task of assessing individual chairs. It is instructive to read these critiques both for what they say and for what they do not say. You will find the chair discussed as a problem in appropriate form, as you would expect. You will find the chair discussed at great length—there are volumes devoted to this—as a problem in materials, as you would also expect. You will find the chair discussed as a problem of architecture—that is, the creation of an independent structure from a variety of materials. You will find the chair discussed as a problem in esthetic statement. You will find it discussed in terms of the effect it has on spaces.

But very rarely do you find a chair discussed as a problem in supporting the human body. That is no minor oversight. Nothing tells us more than this consistent omission, although what it tells us is something we are likely to know already from sitting in chairs that designers have designed. A trade magazine article recently spoke of a revolution in ergonomics. It is awful to think that ergonomics is a novelty in the furniture trade. It's awful just to think of ergonomics, a singularly ugly term used in England to describe an activity that in this country has always been known by a slightly more euphonious—but in connotation even uglier—term: "human engineering."

Whatever it's called, the activity itself is nothing more than an attempt to design a product in a way that takes into account the physical characteristics of the human being who will use the product. This ought not to be a terribly advanced notion. The first man or woman to sit on a rock might not have been conscious of ergonomics, but the first one to turn the rock around until he found its most comfortable surface was. But while designing a chair for the human anatomy ought not to be an uncommon objective, this doesn't mean it is an easy problem. It is not.

The anthropometric drawings on page 50 were done for airplane seating design by the Henry Dreyfuss office. The design of airplane seats is extremely important, because the consumer is literally captive in them. One of the things

The Barcelona chair, the board room chair, Archie Bunker's easy chair—probably most chairs become symbolic. But the meaning of chairs—at least the extent to which chairs can *carry* meaning—is most vividly and mysteriously expressed in the story of the three bears. Dumb animals maybe, but they understood things about design that Goldilocks never dreamed of.

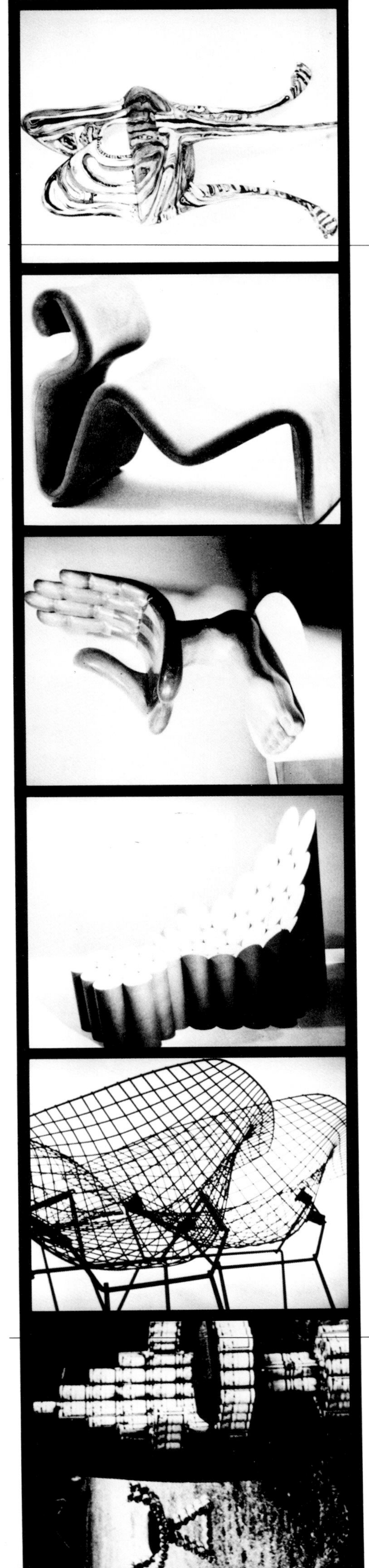

Designers who pride themselves on a disciplined focus upon understanding and forming materials often neglect such materials as flesh and blood—although the flesh is weak and the flow of blood has been greatly impeded by a number of prize-winning chairs.

that the American seats do—at least on some planes—is provide for the extra support that the lumbar region needs. And because not everyone needs the same amount of support, the seatbacks are inflatable. The airline I use most often doesn't know or care about my lumbar region or my ischial tuberosities either, for that matter. Furthermore, to achieve a comfortable lounge appearance, its seats have a unit of extra padding at the top, which has the effect of pushing the head forward. Now, it happens that the head sometimes wants to go forward, but only if it has the option of coming back, which the airline seat does not give it. So your head is not only pushed forward, it is kept there until you reach Saginaw.

Throughout the literature of chair design, whenever structure is spoken of, it is always the chair's structure, never the sitter's structure. Designers who pride themselves on a disciplined focus upon understanding and forming materials, often neglect such materials as flesh and blood—although the flesh is weak and the flow of blood has been greatly impeded by a number of prize-winning chairs.

Staying in one position for too long, which certain chairs encourage, is an insult to the circulatory system, as alcohol is to the liver. I once met a doctor from New York City's St. Vincent's Hospital who as a matter of public duty used to turn over bums that he found sleeping off a drunk or a high—in order to prevent bedsores!

A lot of chairs try to duplicate the contours of the body, but we forget that many of the upholstered chairs seek to duplicate the *composition* of the body. With their frame and springs and stuffing and fabric or leather coverings they are, like us, pretty much made up of skin, bones, wrinkles, and a little fat.

The problem of comfort, of designing a chair with a clear notion of anatomical and circulatory needs, has not been entirely ignored. But it is more likely to be solved in chairs that you might not be comfortable living with for other reasons. The contour chairs and Barcaloungers may not put you in the vanguard of tastemakers, but the manufac-

The materials of chair design range from the base to the exotic. The wilder the imagination, the greater need for constraint. The beer can chair could be monstrous, instead of just funny, and the "scribe's chair" above it could be pretentious instead of elegant, were it not for the fact that in both cases the designers were constrained by the material.

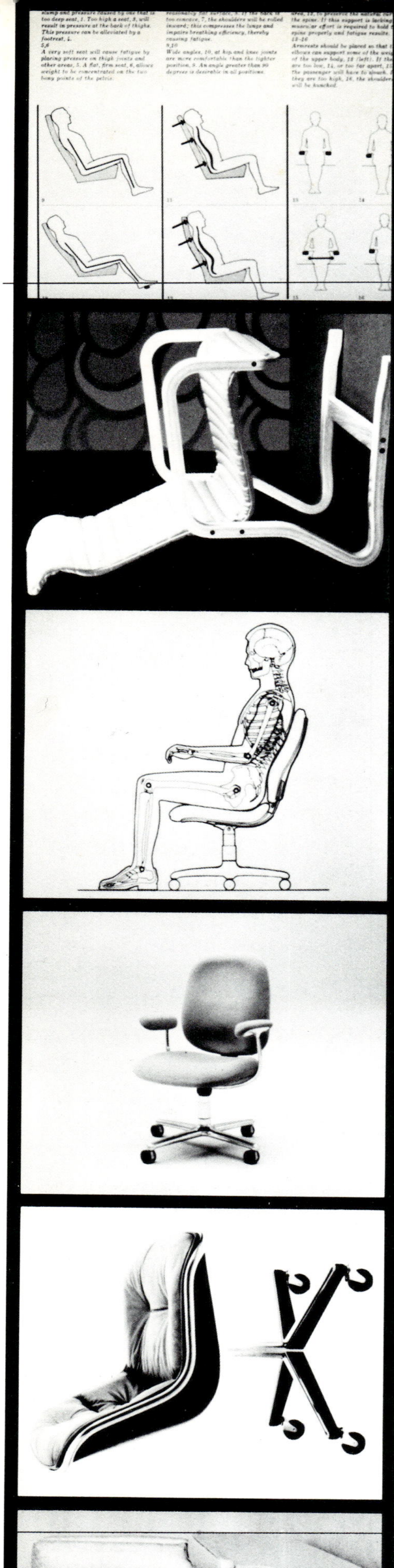

The first man or woman to sit on a rock might not have been conscious of ergonomics, but the first one to turn the rock around until he found its most comfortable surface was.

turers claim their chairs will rest your heart.

Although affluence is associated with sybaritic living, truly comfortable chairs have generally been a middle class achievement. Despite the publicity for the Ergon chair, its concern with physiological requirements of the body is not new. A trade magazine published in 1869 advised that "comfort, convenience and adaptation to health are the chief ends to be secured in the construction of a seat." Ergon advertising copy is strikingly similar. In 1876 the Wilson Adjustable Chair Manufacturing Company in New York advertised a chair designed to alleviate the pains that sedentary workers feel in the small of the back.

Why does this have to be relearned 100 years later? Well, if those who do not know history are condemned to repeat it, it surely is as true in design as anything else. In design, of course, there is a corollary: Those who do know history are privileged to repeat it.

One might wonder whether the Shakers' propensity for shaking is responsible for their excellence in designing and making chairs that rock. Probably not. It seems more reasonably attributable to the sense of proportion that they brought to all their designs, for the rocker is an unusual challenge in proportion. It is very easy to mount a chair on rockers—and very easy to make it look preposterous once it is done. Because of a rocker's essential form, bent wood is the natural material.

Although chairs for general use may have suffered from insufficient attention to function, this is far less true of chairs for special use. That's always the case in design. The artist Saul Steinberg once said, "You always find good design in work things." You don't always, but you are more likely to. If you are working on a farm, milking a cow, fitting someone with shoes, or getting a haircut or a root canal job, you need a particular kind of seat.

What the dentist's chair, the barber's chair, and the electric chair have in common is not just that they are all things we tend to want to avoid, but that the end user is not really the person in the chair but someone else—the operator of the chair. The human needs to be met here are the need of

Not many chairs are designed for the way people are made. This is not surprising, since not many designers know how people are made, or understand the sense in which sitting is an animated, rather than a static, activity. Therapeutic chairs are like therapeutic shoes: neither would be required if chairs and shoes were properly designed in the first place.

the barber for an accessible head and neck and the need of the dentist to see and to work inside the mouth, and the need of both to keep the customer's arms from interfering.

More recently, refinements have been introduced. Now that haircuts cost $25 instead of 25¢, what the customer buys is not just the result—the haircut itself—but the experience, which includes the experience of sitting in a chair that is not only comfortable but at times downright sumptuous. Similarly, dentists have shifted their attention from the mere pulling or filling of teeth to a wide range of services. Psychological consideration becomes important. My own dentist has just collaborated on a book called *Psychodynamics in Dental Practice,* addressed in part to the relationship between the dentist chair and anxiety.

Special-purpose chairs don't always retain their special purposes. The original version of the Hardoy chair was popular as an army officer's campaign chair because of the ease with which it could be folded and moved and unfolded again. Some of the same features made it popular as an American desk chair and as a prop for slapstick comedy.

According to Giedion one of the most powerful elements of ruling taste in the nineteenth century was what he called "the furniture of the engineer." Such furniture included the lounge that converted into a cradle, the bed that converted into a wardrobe, the chair that converted into a lounge, the table chair, the bed chair—a trend that leads ultimately if followed to Ken Isaacs' "Living Chair," more accurately, a live-in chair.

Living may hardly seem to be a special purpose. But designers have often had the impulse to create self-contained environments, and a fairly common fantasy for many of us is that of a bed one never has to leave—a bed in which one can perform almost every human activity except traveling.

The Isaacs chair is not a convertible. It does not open up into or fold up into something else. Instead it is a chair that comes equipped with all of the support paraphernalia that one is likely to bring to it. So what it leaves out is the user's individual design. When you surround a chair with smoking paraphernalia, with food and drink, with a notebook and

Special purpose chairs are almost unfailingly interesting. Since they have to be designed with *some* point in mind, the design is likely to solve an indentifiable problem. The dentist's chair is actually his work environment. He could do without the chairs in his reception room, or in his living room for that matter. But his working chair is essential.

The most compelling special purpose chair I have ever seen is a punitive seat designed to handle unruly inmates at a girl's reform school in Connecticut. Its design is thoroughly evil and superbly detailed. No longer in use as a chair, it serves as a repository for flowers.

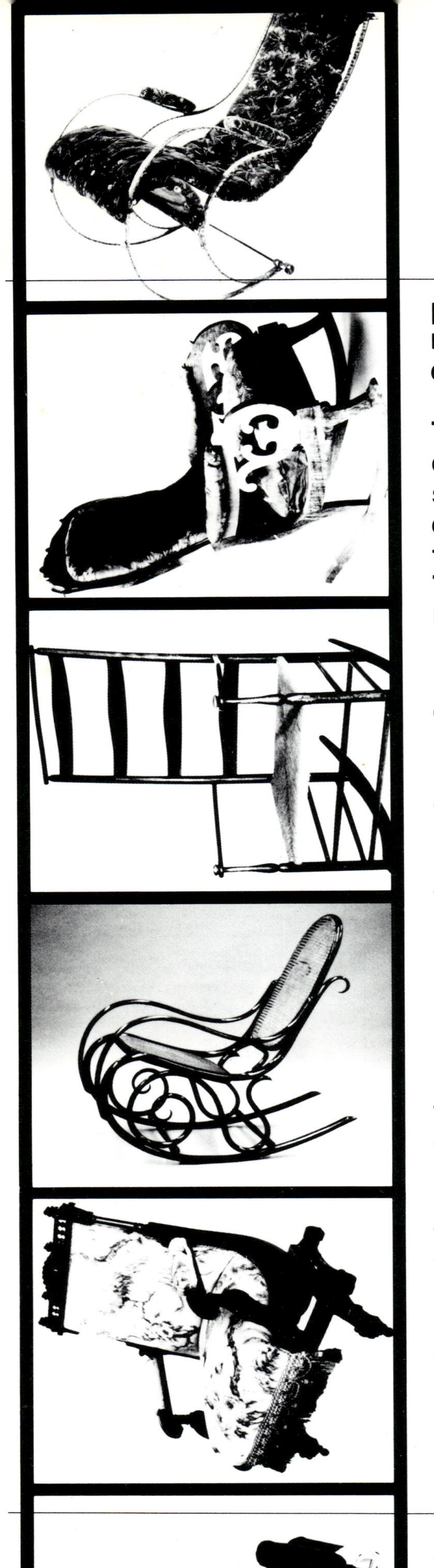

pencil, you are in a very real sense designing your immediate environment. This chair is a self-contained, predesigned immediate environment.

In 1957 the Institute of Design of the Illinois Institute of Technology set out to determine the 100 greatest product designs. They went about it in a rather odd but highly symmetrical way. They selected 100 design experts—designers, critics, writers, teachers—and asked each of them to prepare his or her own list of the ten best designs. Twelve chairs are in the top 100 including the Thonet bentwood chair of 1859, the 1903 director's chair, the 1928 Breuer chair, the 1928 Barcelona chair by Mies van Der Rohe, the 1934 Aalto bent plywood chair, the 1940 Hardoy chair, the 1947 Eames plywood chair, the 1948 Saarinen "Womb," the 1949 Wegner round chair, the Brunswick schoolroom furniture of 1953, the 1957 Eames lounge chair, and the 1957 Saarinen pedestal chair.

Finding so many chairs in a list of the 100 greatest product designs raises anew the question, "Why does it seem to matter so much; what's so special about chairs?"

Well, remember that a chair is not an artifact of service but an artifact of culture. The absence of a chair is a serious cultural deprivation, as the designers of prison and army barracks know.

Remember too that no other animal requires a prosthetic device for regular ongoing use. A chair, after all, is a crutch for a condition that will not mend—walking upright. Designers like to speak of product evolution. But, of course, chairs have not evolved. We have. And once we came down from the trees or up from the sea or whatever—once we gave up the use of four legs for ambulatory purposes, we had to have a prosthetic device to rest on.

Or thought we had to have it. For although a chair is a crutch, it is not a crutch we need physiologically. Perhaps the significance of the chair lies there. It represents the irreducible minimum of the unnecessary. A chair is the first thing you need when you don't really need anything, and is therefore a peculiarly compelling symbol of civilization. For it is civilization, not survival, that requires design.

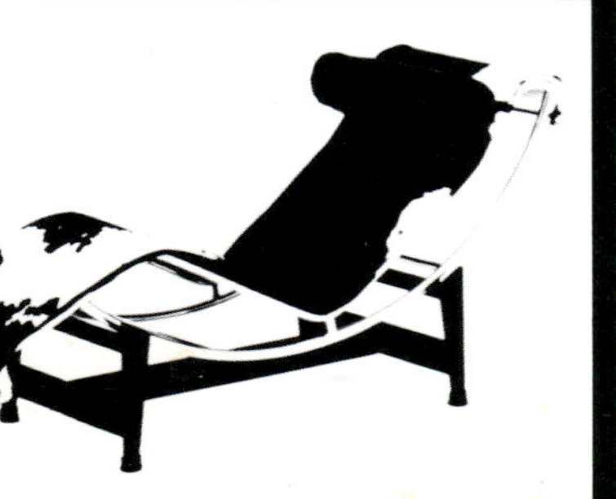

The rocking chair is said to have institutionalized American informality by making native bad manners (leaning back in a chair) acceptable. Although rockers are customarily associated with old people, in fact children love them and our second most vigorous President—John F. Kennedy—rocked by medical prescription.

Mr. Caplan's summary and conclusion to the lecture series "The Evolving Chair" begins on page 100.

Well, remember that a chair is not an artifact of service but an artifact of culture. . . . A chair is the first thing you need when you don't really need anything, and is therefore a peculiarly compelling symbol of civilization.

Photographs on pages 8 and 19 by Michael Pateman.

Bennett

. . . we have become a sitting society over the past 50 years. The shift is greatly a result of our philosophical bent for removing man from labor. We are directing our efforts toward the almost total annihilation of the standing position. A frightening question indeed is: "Who isn't sitting these days?"

The story of the evolving chair began when evolving man found the need to sit and, shortly thereafter, the need to separate his body from the cold, hard, and damp earth. So, man learned to squat at an early age. It is a comfortable and very natural position.

Various squatting stances developed in many societies for specific reasons. They are unique and appropriate manifestations of culture, of body proportions, and of purpose.

In Japan this sitting position is commonly seen even today. There man sits on the ground but for a straw mat, in a style typically associated with Japanese tradition and character. His torso and short legs make this a natural position for his body.

In India, without a chair or stool, men squat this way for hours. It is suited to their thin, small frames and is a comfortable working position for them.

There is also the lotus position for meditation and tranquility. It is one of the most ancient postures. The base of the body forms a triangle from which a vertical line originates, tracing the spine up through the head to the supreme center of psychic power at the

Ward Bennett, designer of castles and penthouses, fashions and office furniture, was born in New York City in 1917. He left home and school in New York at age thirteen to travel extensively throughout Europe and study in Florence and Paris. He has worked with Brancusi, Hans Hoffman, Hattie Carnegie, Louise Nevelson, and Le Corbusier. His sculpture has been exhibited at the Whitney Museum, and his jewelry at the Museum of Modern Art, where some of his work is in the permanent collection. He has been commissioned to design interiors for numerous corporate offices, hospitals and residences, china and glassware for Tiffany and Co., and fabrics and office furniture for Brickel Associates Inc.

top of the skull. This is a position of hatha-yoga which is associated with the intense development of the will, so that all the automatic processes of the body are brought under the control of the mind.

American Indians worked in a squatting position like this (previous page). For them it bespoke a heavier musculature, a physical, active orientation.

The cowboy stance is similar. When he got off his horse in the plains after riding hard all day he assumed this three-point position for relaxation. It suggested his total physicality and a certain alertness to the environment that instinctively remained intact. Relaxing thusly, he meditates on the primeval level of a man unaware that he is meditating.

Let's discuss some reasons for the invention of the first chairs. They came as a practical evolution. Here is a little stool that is made in the jungles of Central and South America. It appears again in Africa and the South Pacific. Notice how it actually lifts the person off the earth. These stools are for the menfolk. As in most primitive societies, the women are left to sit on the ground.

This stool from Colombia is used by the natives for work. I discovered it several years ago when I was visiting there in conjunction with the Save the Children project. We helped these people by building in their huts low wooden platforms covered with straw. We were in fact lifting them off the ground, arthritis being their most crippling disease. This program continues today with amazing success in curtailing the affliction. Our platforms are now seen in schools throughout Central and South America.

The appearance of the table, probably with the development of writing, forced the categorization of chairs into lounge chairs, for rest and comfort, and work chairs, for studying, eating, making a shoe, or creating a piece of jewelry. Even the throne can be placed in the general category of the work chair because it was used not for comfort but for the distinct purpose of designating the authority figure.

With Greek steles, Egyptian sarcophagi, etc., and cross-culturally on through history, statements have been made in art showing the importance of the seated figure—king, deity, hero, dictator. Art-

Hatha Yoga or the "yoga of force" is based on a physiological theory teaching the existence of a dormant internal divine potency. . . . The yogi can control his heartbeat at will, live for days without food and water, and survive for an appreciable length of time even without breathing.

. . . king, diety, hero, dictator . . . sitting is the ultimate position of awe and respect. Today, the great statue of Lincoln in Washington, D.C., is of a seated Lincoln who looks down upon us. God sits.

historically, sitting is the ultimate position of awe and respect. Today, the great statue of Lincoln in Washington, D.C., is of a seated Lincoln who looks down upon us. God sits.

Bucket-type seats appeared in early Egypt. I've seen bas-reliefs and sculptures of them in Delphi as well as actual little terra cotta bucket seats in Athens. They have been made through the ages in everything from straw to stone. These are comfort chairs and, of course, they relate to squatting. Again the squatting position. . . . If you dig a hole in the sand wide enough to fit your hips, then you sit in it and wriggle around, you can create that same bucket kind of pitch. It will be extremely comfortable. You could then pour plaster into the mold and *voilà*—a cast of a bucket seat!

Eighteenth-century Regency chairs are often the bucket type of seat. Also, bucket seats were introduced with some early automobiles. In automobile museums we can see the same design and pitch that we are seeing today in plastic, no different really from Eames or Bertoia. They all feature the holding

The Egyptian chair (above) was created during the XVIII Dynasty, in Thebes, the Valley of the Kings, and is from the tomb of Tut-ankh-amun (courtesy of the Metropolitan Museum of Art, photograph by Harry Burton.)

Most contemporary buckets . . . are too confining, especially the plastic models. They jam you in so that you can hardly cross your legs. . . . A wry comment Frank Lloyd Wright once made about a Saarinen chair: "My God, it's an ass tray."

For the most part, the contemporary seating industry is remarkably negligent about the needs of our bodies. Airplanes are a good example. We are propped and strapped into an angular, uncomfortable position and expected to remain there.

and supporting of the body in a design that works and allows for a certain amount of movement. Most contemporary buckets, however, are too confining, especially the plastic models. They jam you in so that you can hardly cross your legs; integrity has clearly given way to fashion trends. A wry comment Frank Lloyd Wright once made about a Saarinen chair: "My God, it's an ass tray." For the most part, the contemporary seating industry is remarkably negligent about the needs of our bodies. Airplanes are a good example. We are propped and strapped into an angular, uncomfortable position and expected to remain there. And yet, we have become a sitting society over the past 50 years. The shift is greatly a result of our philosophical bent for removing man from labor. We are directing our efforts toward the almost total annihilation of the standing position. A frightening question indeed is: "Who isn't sitting these days?" In Los Angeles one need not walk more than a few steps per day—and for the most part one doesn't—and in a good many places in that city, one just can't.

My interest in chairs stems from a back injury. I hurt myself seriously many years ago skiing and was hospitalized for a while. After this I made the rounds of doctors, searching out one who could help free me from repeated back spasms. Finding a doctor is like finding a good auto mechanic—very difficult.

Eventually there were two doctors who helped me. One was Dr. Howard Rusk, of the Institute of Rehabilitation at New York University, who helped me, through exercise, to solve my lower lumbar problem, and later I happily and fortunately met Dr. Janet Travell, who worked with President Kennedy for many years. She is an extraordinary woman, and she taught me how to sit and what to look for in a chair. I had had no idea about seating until after we met. She developed proportions very different from those in the chairs that were then available. Basically, she advocated a short seat with support of the lower lumbar region, much in contrast to one of the speakers in this lecture series who indicates that sitting on the edge of the chair is ideal. I learned that it is best to sit back into the chair, that is, to sit *in* and not *on* a chair, and also that there should be arms on

the chair. I believe arms are second in importance only to proper lumbar support.

In Zen Buddhist meditation it is possible to train oneself to control both the mind and the breathing and to manage to sit still, comfortably, for long periods, even weeks. We, in contrast, are a tense and fidgety society. We don't know how to sit and we don't know how to sit still. If you observe the audience in a moving picture theater, you will see a twisting and turning and slouching that never end—evidence that we have not been taught to sit properly. Chair design has contributed to the problem. The chairs you are sitting in now are an example; you can't move in them. They are confining and, for me, very uncomfortable, limiting, and binding. Of course, there cannot be a perfect chair. How could one seat accommodate a seven-pound babe and a 170-pound adult, a five-foot woman and a six-foot-six man? Impossible.

There are some basic proportions however—certain heights, depths, heights of arms—that can work. Although my reputation rests on designs pared

"You wouldn't dream of buying shoes that don't fit you. But have you ever stopped to consider whether the chairs you sit in are right for you?. . . one can go into most homes and *not find a single chair that's properly designed to support the framework of the human body. . . .*"
—Dr. Janet Travell, "Chairs Are a Personal Thing", *House Beautiful,* October, 1955.

In Zen Buddhist meditation it is possible to train oneself to control both the mind and the breathing and to manage to sit still, comfortably, for long periods, even weeks. We in contrast are a tense and fidgety society. We don't know how to sit and we don't know how to sit still.

Ideally, of course, (chairs) should be made in sizes; the Victorians had a grandfather, grandmother, and child's chair. Even more importantly, chairs should be made to order. We could make figure casts. . . .

down to the simplest denominator, I suggest that what success I have achieved comes not from design originality but from the concept of comfort. My chairs are installed in large numbers all over the country. In them a man or a woman can find reasonable comfort—unusual, for not many humanized chairs exist.

The basic proportional height of the chair relates to the distance from the heel to the knees. Ideally, of course, chairs should be made in sizes; the Victorians had a grandfather, grandmother, and child's chair. Even more importantly, chairs should be made to order. We could make figure casts and analyze the various dimensions. My elbow height, for example, is six-and-a-half inches from the seat. Someone with a longer arm would obviously be much more comfortable if the chair arm were adjusted to fit his larger frame. Getting in and out of a chair is also critically important, most especially in hospitals and for the aged. So, returning to the point I mentioned earlier about arms, they should be high and very sturdy so that a person can use them to lift himself. For the

"Specialization is the heartache of society in many ways. Design has become so limited that purses or belt buckles can become a designer's whole life's work. I think the limits are bad both for the designers and the designs. Why, for example, should automotive design be so linked to Detroit and leave us stuck with such lousy automobiles?"—Bennett

"The chair, like writing, appears as a sign of civilization. . . . Used first by the elders or wise men of a community who needed to relax in a sitting position, chairs soon became a symbol of importance and this naturally led to their embellishment."—Marvin D. Schwartz, *Please Be Seated,* The American Federation of Arts, 1968.

A chair should provide the means to satisfy the body's need for a position change. There should be no reason why you cannot throw your leg over the arm of a chair. When on a long plane flight, I spend a third of the journey walking around or standing, just to break the physical insult of that jackknife position.

aged, especially, it is important that the back legs of a chair do not extend beyond the back of the chair so they may be tripped over, and rubber discs should be placed on each foot of the chair to prevent sliding.

Whether sitting, standing, or lying down, we cannot remain in one position for long; we are not built to be stationary. When bedridden, we may get bedsores. Exercise and movement are extremely important. A chair should provide the means to satisfy the body's need for a position change. There should be no reason why you cannot throw your leg over the arm. When on a long plane flight, I spend a third of the journey walking around or standing, just to break the physical insult of that jackknife position.

This of course is a rocker. The idea of a rocker . . . and of a gout stool . . . is to enable you to find your most comfortable pitch. The length of my legs determines their most comfortable angle of extension. In a sitting position there are certain proportions of the legs which determine whether the knees should be positioned at a 90-, 100-, or 135-degree angle. It is very important that there be no pressure on the muscles and vessels at the back of the knee. If these are pinched by the chair, extreme discomfort follows.

When I sit this way in this rocker I achieve perfect pitch, or perfect lower lumbar back support for myself. That makes this chair more comfortable than existing commercial chairs ostensibly built for comfort, particularly the overstuffed chairs. They feel good because they are soft, but the body compensates for lack of lumbar support by putting strain on other muscles, and so the good feeling soon gives way to muscle tension and even pain.

I own a Brighton beachchair, made in England more than 100 years ago. When I got it, it was covered with fringe and tassels. I think that it has one of the most comfortable pitches that I have ever found. We have all done this, finding a chair that has a pitch that best supports our lower lumbar region.

If you have a bad back, and so many Americans do, it is very important to understand that you can help yourself to be more comfortable and to sit more correctly by strengthening your stomach muscles and hamstrings. This relates to two basic tenets for

Bennett's 2001 U-Chair (top right), available from Brickel Associates Inc., New York City.

those of us with lower lumbar disc problems: Never arch your back, because arching the back pinches the vertabrae. And: Always keep your stomach in, because in this way a rounded back posture is achieved, which again provides the lower lumbar support position offered by a properly pitched chair. If you pull in your stomach you cannot arch your back. The same holds true if you place your foot on a bar rail. The back doesn't arch when your foot is held up in this position. The bar rail has real meaning. To wit: Why do so many people have spasms while brushing their teeth? Because their backs are arched.

For anyone interested in designing chairs, the procedure should start with the pitch. Here is a chair I have designed, using the pitch inspired by my old Brighton chair. It is an approach I often take—finding a chair that is comfortable, taking a pattern of the pitch, and then making another chair, which usually turns out to be a much simplified version. Note that this chair doesn't have arms—very rare for me.

The student of chair design will notice that form

"I think the business end eats up a designer's creativity, and yet, it's terribly hard to work without someone to produce the designs. If you want to do a movie, you have to find a producer."—Bennett

. . . form and proportion haven't changed much over the years. The cruciform leg of the Barcelona chair appears in Egyptian folding stools, Greek metal furniture. . . . Technology has introduced the steam-bending of wood, metal tubing, spring steel, plastics, foam, inflatables—but nevertheless, a chair is a chair is a chair.

and proportion haven't changed much over the years. The cruciform leg of the Barcelona chair appears in Egyptian folding stools, Greek metal furniture, and the folding leather and steel military version Napoleon carried along on his campaigns. Technology has introduced the steam-bending of wood, metal tubing, spring steel, plastics, foam, inflatables—nevertheless, a chair is a chair is a chair.

These are only a few of my designs. There are 150 at the showroom. They are always pared down to the minimum—no tricks, nothing clever. I have no interest in making chairs that look like baseball gloves or hands or that are gilded—but I am interested in chairs that are comfortable for human bodies. If the comfort and function are right, then it follows that the esthetics will be good. A working structure simply has to be beautiful. Corbu's statement "Start with the inside" symbolically relates to our own human skeletal structure—without this element of function it falls apart, becomes clever, amusing, but beautiful? I don't think so.

The 1098 Scissor chair, the 1074 round carved-wood frame arm chair (top right), and the 1124 carved-wood frame arm chair, available from Brickel Associates Inc., New York City.

"You can't design a chair on paper so I create a cardboard pattern, full-size, and then add forms and shapes out of muslin or bamboo that I can stick on and take off, the way a fashion designer works with a dummy."—Bennett

I have no interest in making chairs that look like baseball gloves or hands or that are gilded—but I am interested in chairs that are comfortable for human bodies. If the comfort and function are right, then it follows that the esthetics will be good.

The 1132 Low-Arm side chair (top), and the 1550 University carved-wood frame arm chair (above). The 1502 Turtle Back series (upper right), and the 1223 carved-wood frame arm chair (lower right). All available from Brickel Associates Inc., New York City.

"Ward Bennett has created 96 designs for Brickel. These are produced and sold at an average of 30,000 units annually."—Stephen Brickel, Executive Vice President, Brickel Associates, Inc.

The most recent Bennett design, his 2412 Alexandria Chair, was inspired by Egyptian Temple architecture at Luxor. It has a hand-carved white ash frame with a sled base and is fully upholstered, using textiles designed by Bennett. Available at Brickel Associates Inc., New York City. All photographs by Michael Pateman.

D'Urso

The standardization and conventionalizing of seating is a problem. Go to Bloomingdale's, or any other store, and notice the number of conventional chairs and sofas. These provide us with all the evidence we need to realize that in terms of furniture, people have been conditioned. There are a few designers working in other directions, however, challenging the conventional attitudes governing furniture within space. They are concerned with an abstract view of seating.

A child, during a day's play, naturally assumes more resting attitudes and positions than an adult. His imagination, freedom from conventional thinking, and greater body awareness and flexibility allow this. I believe that we, as adults, still crave the informality and variety of childhood. Nature serves as the common denominator. My aim is to create an interior landscape, a friendly and inviting terrain that permits and even encourages spontaneous, casual exploration of the horizontal plane. I take my notes from the ways the outdoor landscape on a summer day allows for various intimate and satisfying body contacts—perching on a railing or ledge, lying, leaning against a tree or a rock. These same sensations can be created in an interior by designing different levels and edges as well as other varied surfaces.

We can begin with the basic concept of sitting on the floor, something we all have done. My feeling is that a floor should be an inviting surface to sit upon. If you don't sit on it, there is a reason, and that is because the surface isn't inviting. In other words, things happen because they're allowed to happen.

Most of the living spaces that I design are carpeted. When all surfaces are available to be experienced—lain upon, sat on, worked on—a sense of total environment forms. I have found that commercial (tightly woven) carpet is the best material to use for covering platforms and other tactile surfaces and is the key to the success of this approach. It is pleasant to the touch, relatively easy to maintain, visually unassuming, firm yet adequately cushioned. Pile carpets, on the other hand, are usually too soft, don't wrap well, and are difficult to maintain, while natural floor coverings such as sisal are too rough on the skin. When this kind of atmosphere is established on the floor, people feel free to extend the precedent further, perhaps to sitting on the back of something like the sofa or the banquette. The upward progression leads to still other levels and other experiences. By introducing intermediate levels through the use of elements that become seating—banquettes or viewing platforms, for example—we offer a break with tradition. We are no longer resorting to standardized furniture units or "objects" (which is what they are) in a room. The architectural volume improves with the integration of the new dimensions, designed as an actual part of the space. What is important is the basic difference in approach, transforming a space versus filling it with objects. This approach to seating enables us to create a unique sitting area, one that exists as part of a greater whole, as opposed to a series of different parts.

I am also interested in the idea of sitting on stools, because they are easy to pull around with you and they provide the opportunity to sit briefly without a particular direction imposed. A stool is such a minimal thing. It leads me to the idea of using casters or wheels. These would allow you to move easily to the area where you want to be. It is good that some of the seating in a room is not fixed to a particular location.

The stool also brings another situation to mind. People really seem to enjoy sitting on ladders even though they probably don't do it very often. Everybody paints walls at one time or another. When you climb the ladder and you're sitting up there looking down into the room, you experience a new view of the space. When you're relatively high up, looking down into a room, you get a perspective that you wouldn't get by sitting on conventional furniture, especially if you are so high that you're unable to stand without touching the ceiling. You can lean on walls and

Joe D'Urso, born in 1945, leads the sophisticated, pragmatic, and very minimalist movement in interiors that is becoming the lexicon for New York's East Side. The combination of his general philosophy and thorough grounding in interior design, begun as an architecture and interior design student at Pratt (five years), and the Royal College of Art and Manchester Polytechnic in England, had produced by 1974 an oeuvre selected for a one-man show at the Museum of Modern Art, New York. After this he began a professional association with Ward Bennett, and in 1968 set out to found his own firm, D'Urso Design, in New York. His work received the Burlington Outstanding Young Designer Award in 1973.

My aim is to create an interior landscape, a friendly and inviting terrain that permits and even encourages spontaneous, casual exploration of the horizontal plane. I take my notes from the ways the outdoor landscape on a summer day allows for various intimate and satisfying body contacts—perching on a railing or ledge, lying, leaning against a tree or a rock.

People really seem to enjoy sitting on ladders even though they probably don't do it very often. . . . When you climb the ladder and you're sitting up there looking down into the room, you experience a new view of the space. . . . You can lean on walls and sit on floors, but how often do people get a chance to touch the ceiling?

Photographs on page 33 by Duane Michals; pages 34, 35, 36 (right), 40, and 41 by Peter Aaron; pages 36 (left), 38 (left), and 39 by Michael Datoli; and pages 37, and 38 (right) by Richard Champion.

. . . surely the center portion of a three-seater sofa is an awkward and unsettling place to be. Breaking up a long seating element into defined areas by the usual method of butting separate cushions together creates an unfortunate formality, a sense of rigidity, and a psychology that is inappropriate to domestic activity.

sit on floors, but how often do people get a chance to touch the ceiling? Once it happened to me (by accident, at that, in a space I designed), I felt it was such a wonderful experience that I've reconsidered again.

I use a heading called "Serious Seating" when I talk about conventional solutions to problems. I always start with the sofa. As I mentioned before, I think people are conditioned to conventional furniture ideas. The sofa is the perfect illustration of this. It has become the key to the sitting area in the living room; its validity as a practical object or the psychology it sets up goes unquestioned. The pleasant side of sofas in the past—generous depth and scale, the softness of down, good craftsmanship—has degenerated, the result of standardization, economics, and style. The modern sofa consists of hard-edge and unyielding (physically and visually) foam cushions of shallow depth. Usually, the craftsmanship is poor. And surely, the center portion of a three-seater sofa is an awkward and unsettling place to be. Breaking up a long seating element into defined areas by the usual method of butting separate cushions together creates an unfortunate formality, a sense of rigidity, and a psychology that is inappropriate to domestic activity. The problems with these sofas are compounded with the tendency to push them back to the wall. An element that should visually be three-dimensional becomes attached to, and so closely associated with, the wall that you lose all awareness of the back of it. This, in turn, radically changes the proportions of the room in the sense that the line where the floor hits the wall is erased, along with the distinct proportions of the wall and the floor. It's really amazing to watch what happens when you move everything away from the wall. When pulled into the middle of the room, these furnishings are expressed as objects unable to change the proportions of anything. It is the placement of these objects then that makes the incredible difference in the ways we perceive the architectural volume of interior spaces.

When dealing with apartments that are not particularly good architecturally, having serious problems regarding window positions, air-conditioning or heating units, or pipes in impossible places, etc., I try to use the elements of seating to transform the architecture and thereby solve the problems. This is where the whole idea of platforms and banquettes comes in. With these we are able to create a new floor, perhaps at the height of a window sill, and while it remains the floor it also becomes the sofa, or fills other functional requirements—for eating, sleeping, storage, etc. This concept belongs to a completely different visual vocabulary from the old sofa/object orientation. These elements exist as abstract parts when not in use, fulfilling another role as part of the architectural totality of space, only taking on a separate reality when responding to a more particular usage.

My observations have led me to accept the idea of designing a room that is basically a room to be sat in. I mean this in terms of heights—

heights of windows, grills, expressions of mechanical systems, the height at which paintings are hung or a piece of sculpture is placed. I think it makes more sense to relate to the scale of sitting and to design the living space in terms of eye level in sitting positions than to relate to the scale of standing attitudes. In most rooms, as soon as you sit down everything seems too high and you get this very unsettling feeling of the proportion of the space. This may seem subtle or irrelevant to some, but to my way of thinking these considerations can radically change the environment.

I have become increasingly aware of what a chair actually is and why one would have a chair in a space. There seems to be a situation where a chair, as well as being a place to sit, is also purely and simply an object in space, a visual experience. And in this sense it could become a metaphor for art, or a source of inspiration. A chair can be an indication, more even to yourself than to others, of your own attitudes toward de-

Alvar Aalto, a Finnish architect, designed the Scroll Armchair in 1934. He fabricated the materials for most of his chair designs by himself. They consisted of simple plywood and came to be known only as Aalto chairs. The Scroll chair is manufactured by Artek (Finland) and is available from International Contract Furnishings, New York City.

There seems to be a situation where a chair, as well as being a place to sit, is also purely and simply an object in space, a visual experience. And in this sense it could become a metaphor for art, or a source of inspiration.

sign, materials, or technology—that kind of statement.

What I'd like to do now is to use slides to show you particular jobs and describe some of the problems and how I solved them.

This was a radical conversion of a suburban house in Sands Point, Long Island. I was trying to get as much daylight into the space as possible because there was a large overhang over the west wall, which was the window wall. The area is quite large but dark during the day. So I introduced two skylights that go across the roof in front of the window wall to bring in light, brightening the space.

I have attempted to give the idea of a sofa without actually having one. It's a played-down experience of sofa. The important things about it are, first, its being a window seat, where you would have a view; and, second, the informal design, which invites you to lie back, or whatever. The thing in detail here that I attempted was to eliminate separation between the elements—the material of the sofa and the outside. A large sheet of thermopane twelve feet wide and the brown leather sofa were designed so that the glass slotted right into the back of the sofa, and the leather just wrapped around.

I don't know how many of these chairs you're familiar with, but these two in the middleground are Aalto chairs, lounge chairs in laminated wood. For the dining chairs, we put together a collection of original Thonet bentwood chairs, none of which is the same. And again here is an idea—a bed, a kind of daybed that I had made which is positioned under the skylight. When you lie back you're able to look up and see clouds and stars.

When you do a banquette, or when you do any large upholstered element in a room, what kind of chair works best with it? My feelings are that it should be a chair you can drag around pretty easily and fairly dissimilar visually from the upholstered pieces; it should be linear and less bulky and less upholstered. There are very few

There are very few chairs that I like—I mean I could name them on one hand—the few very good chairs. Some of the chairs designed by Mies, Corbu, and Breuer and a few others I don't mind using over and over again.

chairs that I like—I mean I could name them on one hand—the few very good chairs. Some of the chairs designed by Mies, Corbu, and Breuer and a few others I don't mind using over and over again. This brings up an interesting point. I think you have to be careful *not* to deny yourself certain things just because other people have them. Basically, it's not so much the object, in this case the chair, that matters; it's the environment, the total environment. The way a chair would look in a room rather than in another room may be worlds apart.

This is an apartment in the city that was done about five years ago. I used the same Aalto chair, again here an attempt to eliminate a sofa from the space and to create an element that could give the room a kind of anchor, a focal point, a character that it didn't have before. This seemed necessary because we didn't do any structural work.

The platform is completely free-standing so that you can sit on either side and it's a place for a guest to stay over. I think the platform is 12 inches high and the pad is about 4 inches, so it ends up approximately 16 inches high, typical sofa height. There are just a few chairs, and these are secretarial chairs on wheels. I only believe in the comfortable, upholstered chairs used singly, as for reading, or in a grouping without a banquette.

This is another suburban house, in Great Neck. I used a sofa because these are older clients, and although people of all ages can relate to the platforms, the floor as a surface for sitting or reclining is essentially a contemporary phenomenon; it relates to the surge of interest in body conditioning and improvement. I felt that it would be better to give these people seating that would support them more. Even when there are two people sitting on a sofa you have a little bit of space left between them; you could even work your way into a corner. The relationship of these sofas to the table facing the fireplace shows the room's geometric orientation.

Here is an intentional attempt to minimize the

"That many architects like Corbu, Breuer, Aalto, and Mies . . . have devoted so much time to furniture design may be puzzling. The reasons are twofold: first, no modern architect believes that interior design can be separated from exterior design. The inside and the outside of a modern structure are regarded as one, thanks to the technological development of building with large sheets of glass, and the aesthetic development of sensing objects simultaneously from many vantage points. And, second, most modern architects have found chairs and tables to be excellent guinea pigs on which to experiment, simply and directly, with certain aesthetic and technical concepts."—Peter Blake, *The Master Builders.* Alfred A. Knopf, Inc., New York, 1970.

When you have separate cushions every 2 feet or so you get a feeling of being told where to sit; you can't sit anywhere and everywhere, because you have to avoid sitting on a split. This may be okay for waiting rooms, but not for homes.

material difference between the table and the chair. Look at the way the table edge picks up and reflects the chairs around it, something I like very much.

Another thing that I've noticed (and again it's a subtlety, but I think it has a tremendous psychological implication) is the way most sofas, and even banquettes, actually divide into segments, making for specific places to sit. When you have separate cushions every 2 feet or so you get a feeling of being told where to sit; you can't sit anywhere and everywhere, because you have to avoid sitting on a split. This may be okay for waiting rooms, but not for homes. And when you sit alone on this big unit, or share it with one other person, you are occupying one section while all the others remain empty. So I've experimented with an uninterrupted cushion 15 feet long. One continuous surface 36 inches deep, or deeper, with many loose back pillows, rather than bolsters, allows you to create your own little nest, your own little area, and you find a comfortable pitch. Or you can take the pillows off and throw them on the floor. They look fine wherever they end up because you don't feel they're missing from anywhere else.

Question: What's the banquette made of?

D'Urso: Plywood. It's constructed as a floor would be constructed; as a matter of fact, the whole area under that platform is storage for suitcases and files and things. So it really becomes a basement.

Question: How do you get into the storage area?

D'Urso: Well, you get in from the back, right through the slit on the side with the firewood in it. There are panels that you can crawl through. You can't stand under it, but you can crawl. It's about 40″ high. It's nice because I think in a way it illustrates what I've been trying to say. Any person at any given moment can just invent his own place and way of sitting there. And it lends itself to unrestricted movement. The whole thing is casual, spontaneous, and abstract.

This is in a New York City apartment building that was innovative in that it was built so that it

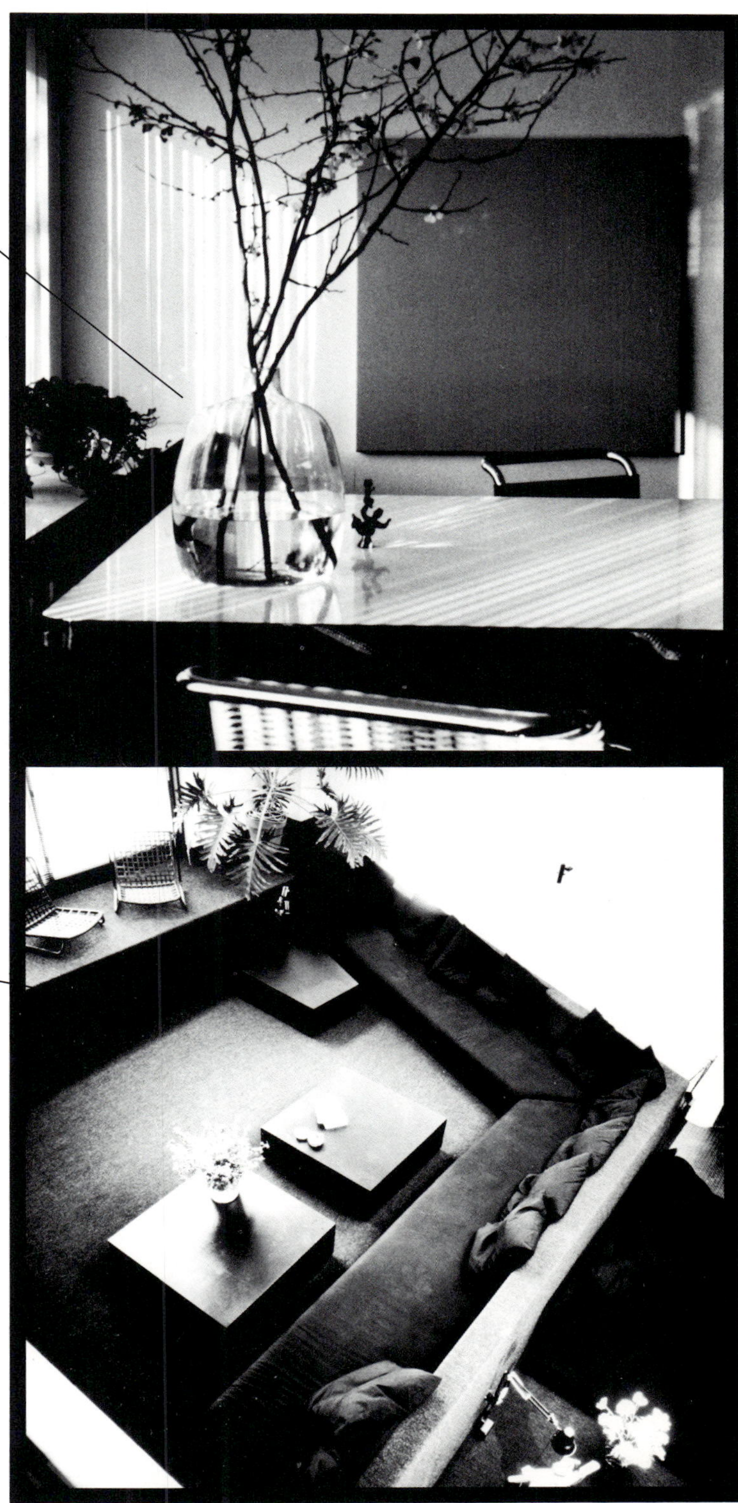

Any person at any given moment can just invent his own place and way of sitting there. And it lends itself to kind of unrestricted movement. The whole thing is casual, spontaneous, and abstract.

could be one large space or partitioned to create a separate bedroom. The client, who was 19 at the time, had just dropped out of design school. This was the first environment he could call his own. He was a very interesting client to work with because he had a lot to do with designing the space.

The wide, low platform across the windows is one step up, about 8 inches. It is an attempt to change the proportions, to stretch out, to accentuate the long and narrow. The nicest thing about this apartment was that the windows were on the long end, as opposed to the short end. People are used to going into a space and seeing windows on the short end. Raising the platform up those 8 inches makes the windowsill that much lower, so when you're sitting on the platform you get more sense of looking out.

Question: How much does it cost to transform a room like this?
D'Urso: What difference does it make?

Question: Well, I'm curious. It's the one subject that, of all of this stuff, I'm really curious about. I'm *dying* to know what the guy paid for this. Do I have to give you a reason why? I think it's pretty obvious why. I'm just damn curious how much all this cost the young fellow.
D'Urso: Well, I don't think it has anything to do with it. Unless one goes into it in detail, it doesn't——
Question: Just an overall figure of what it cost this person.
D'Urso: I once got into trouble telling somebody (in public)——
Question: I don't want you to get into trouble!
D'Urso: It even got very awkward.
Question: $3000, $4000, $5000?
D'Urso: Well, you know the chair is an expensive chair, about $900.

The table, which I had made, was $1000. Those lights, because they were prototypes at that time, I think cost about $50 each to make. But you could use another light, in fact, that costs $20. I've even used much cheaper chairs. I mean, that could be a canvas beach chair; it might even be nicer for someone. And the table could be a 4-by-8 flush door, I suppose. Formally, it would function in the same way—a slab is all it is. It doesn't really make any difference whether it's expensive or not. Well, sometimes it does make a difference, but I think ultimately not an important one. What is either good or not good about it is the contrast from the space in which there was a problem. When we minimized the elements in terms of numbers and maximized them in terms of scale, did we create a successful environment?
Question: How much?
D'Urso: It depends on who does it and how you do it. If you did it yourself, or had a friend do it, you could do it *so* cheaply. But if you have—
Question: But——
D'Urso: I think that was $3000 to do all the construction. The total apartment as you see it, furnished, carpeted, etc., was something like $10,000.

"For two thousand years classical design has been a prime source of inspiration. In spite of all the technological and philosophical innovations, will the break from the classical tradition be permanent? Chair design reflects attitudes that are much more complex than just sitting."—Marvin D. Schwartz, *Please Be Seated,* The American Federation of Arts, 1968.

My feeling is that a floor should be an inviting surface to sit upon. If you don't sit on it, there is a reason, and that is because the surface isn't inviting.

Diffrient

The sad picture of Mr. Average—always bent in the middle like a kinked garden hose (with a similar loss of circulation). His condition worsens with his lack of exercise. His muscles lack tone. He hasn't the ability to hold his body in a good posture for long periods while sitting.

Chair design is the acid test for designers. A chair design should provide a good-looking, functional seat that is comfortable. Comfort in a chair involves the spine, neck and head, thighs and buttocks. Comfort, then, is a rather unsolvable problem, so many designers ignore it altogether and deal with form alone, thereby producing incomplete products.

FIRST LECTURE: The position we call sitting may not necessarily be a posture our maker intended for us. Many of our physical ailments are by-products of sitting. Sitting is to be thought of as a compromise position since man in his natural habitat functions best when he is either erect and moving or supine and resting. Sitting is a cultural by-product. In many ways it counters the natural balance of physical man and his surroundings.

The kinds of sitting can be seen as almost universally the direct result of social or cultural habits or conditions. Sitting is useful when we do certain kinds of work. It also provides a modicum of rest while we remain alert. We tend to overlook that some tasks, such as creative thinking, might be better performed when lying down, or a job such as drafting might be best done standing. Be that as it may, all evidence indicates that ours has become a sit-down culture. The average man spends as much as two hours (sometimes more) commuting behind the wheel of an automobile or in a train. This is followed by roughly eight hours behind a desk or operating a machine. And after this day of sitting, what happens?—an evening spent sitting watching TV.

Think a moment about the kinds of chairs used daily by the average man. There are the seats in the car or train which he occupies while the vehicle is bouncing or jostling along. These seats generally provide poor body support, and the bouncing simply aggravates the situation. At the desk or machine there are chairs that give reasonable support, but for the most part they are less than satisfactory. Then, finally, at day's end there is the big, soft, overstuffed living room chair, and this is the worst of all.

The sad picture of Mr. Average—always bent in the middle like a kinked garden hose (with a similar loss of circulation). His condition worsens with his lack of exercise. His muscles lack tone. He hasn't the ability to hold his body in a good posture for long periods while sitting. However, to use the muscles exclusively for body support, without the aid of a properly designed chair, would fatigue even an athlete.

Chair design is the acid test for designers. A chair design should provide a good-looking, functional seat that is comfortable. Comfort in a chair involves the spine, neck and head, thighs and buttocks. Comfort, then, is a rather unsolvable problem, so many designers ignore it altogether and deal with form alone, thereby producing incomplete products. This, I feel, is not good design. Comfort cannot be incidental. This is my view; there is a great deal of controversy on the subject.

A great deal of my time is spent setting up standards of comfort for chairs. The standards are arrived at through data accumulated by the testing of actual seated people. Next week my talk will be concerned with the various devices we have created to gather our comfort information. The remainder of tonight's time will be spent in, I hope, an interesting way. I am going to ask you to test chairs found in today's marketplace and to rate them from one to ten on the basis of their comfort for your individual body. A rating of ten is the most comfortable. In each case, we will rate the chair while wearing a blindfold, and after the score is recorded, the blindfold will be removed and the chair rated again. The results of the tests ought to tell us something about chair comfort, how it varies according to individuals, and how our perception gets in the way of what our body tells us.

SECOND LECTURE: Our effort last week was to bring out something more than just the scientific aspects of comfort and also to show that there really is no agreement on comfort. In spite of this, it is possible to find some references and some fairly extensive studies on what provides an individual comfort in a seated position.

TEST # 1: Because of the differences in the shapes of individuals, there probably can be no universal agreement on comfort and what it is.

However, the tests, which I've had a chance to go over a little more carefully during the week, show some consistencies. [See overleaf.] For instance, a really uncomfortable chair, like that folding chair, was generally rated quite low whether the person was blindfolded or not. That's no big surprise. Other chairs that come close to what the experts say comfort is in chairs were rated rather high. To some degree, that kind of consistency tends to confirm what experts are telling us about seated comfort. Tonight we'll go into that in varying degrees. We will show how the standards are developed.

The interesting thing in the blindfold test is how remarkably consistent you were. For the most part, there were no broad-spread contradictions

Niels Diffrient was born in Mississippi in 1929, educated at Wayne University and Cranbrook Academy of Art, and was a Fulbright fellow in design and Architecture in 1954. His design activities include teaching, lecturing, consulting, and writing. Perhaps he is best known for his work on *Humanscale 1/2/3,* for which he received a government award citing its contribution to studies on the handicapped. He is now a partner in the firm Henry Dreyfuss Associates/Industrial Designers, New York. He specializes in products for transportation and the utilities industry, furniture design, medical equipment, industrialized architecture, interiors and graphics. He is considered a leading expert in airplane seat design.

All in all, the only thing I can say is that, very pointedly, nobody knows what they're talking about. I hope that's an exaggeration, but nevertheless, the rating shows how comfort is a very subjective thing.

between when you couldn't and when you could see the chair. That's somewhat counter to test results I've seen published elsewhere.

But there were some spreads in the test results and they are interesting. For instance, that Saarinen Tulip chair, the white chair on the pedestal base, is quite a handsome chair. Its comfort rating went up in three instances and down only once when the blindfolds were removed. But one person rated it so low in comfort that even after removing the blindfold its average stayed virtually the same, 5.8. Generally, however, these statistics tend to confirm that some chairs because of their looks convince you that they are more comfortable than they really are.

There are other interesting things I've seen happen before—for instance, the transparent folding chair that I mentioned earlier most often is upgraded in this test. It usually tends to get a better grade because it has such a flashy look. Only one person in our test dramatically upped his grade after removing his blindfold and as a result the comfort average remained low. Notice how low it is. Nobody found it comfortable throughout both tests, that in turn confirms for me the documentation of comfort.

But the champagne chair, the one that looks like the white pedestal in a clear material, would normally be expected to get a higher grade after you saw it. But it didn't. None of you was fooled by that. That chair sold very well when Plexiglas was the "in" thing to sit in; you could see your backsides from any point in the room. So again, in every case the average doesn't reflect much spread even if one or two people marked a dramatic rating one way or another.

TEST #2: This test, conducted without blindfolds and using another set of chairs, really flew in every direction. This may have been because there were quite different chairs; they varied greatly one from the other.

The Barcelona chair on the whole got the highest average, which is rather remarkable considering the variation in your bodies. Somebody should have been uncomfortable in that chair; yet, you see, its comfort remained remarkably consistent.

However, if you are going to do any designing, in my opinion, you can't really approach comfort as a subjective thing. That's how it has been approached in the past and as a result chairs aren't that good. When they are considered good they're mostly just good-looking, not good to sit in. Anybody who designs a chair really ought to know what he's designing. I doubt very seriously that if an engineer were going to design an engine he would get very far if he based his model only upon subjective ratings of performance. He has to be pretty accurate or the engine won't work. The same is true of a chair. Despite its built-in tolerance, or compensation, the chair must be made to serve a purpose; it must work.

Tested: the Tulip Pedestal Chair, designed by Eero Saarinen in 1956–57. Fiberglass shell, cast aluminum base with plastic finish, and a wool zippered cover on foam rubber cushion. Available from Knoll International, New York City.

Tested: the Eames DCM Chair, designed by Charles Eames in 1946. Chromium plated tubular steel frame, formed plywood seat and back. Available from Herman Miller. Photographs by Charles Eames.
Tested: the Prague Chair, designed by Josef Hoffman in 1925. Steam bent beechwood frame, cane seat and back. Available from Stendig International, New York.

Tested: the Barcelona Chair, designed by Mies van der Rohe in 1929. Chromium nickel-plated steel bar frame, with saddle leather straps and leather cushions.
Tested: the Wassily Chair, designed by Marcel Breuer in 1925. Made with a chromium nickel-plated steel frame, and a leather seat, back and sides. Both available from Knoll International, New York City.

Anybody who designs a chair really ought to know what he's designing. I doubt very seriously that if an engineer were going to design an engine he would get very far if he based his model only upon subjective ratings of performance. He has to be pretty accurate or the engine won't work.

TEST #1	Participants 1	2	3	4	5	6	7	8	9	10	11	Average
1. Saarinen Tulip												
With blindfold	6			8				7	7	4	3	5.8
Without blindfold	6			—				9	8	5	1	5.8
2. Eames Plywood												
With blindfold		3	5		5	3	8					4.8
Without blindfold		3	6		8	4	6					5.4
3. "Plia" Folding												
With blindfold		2	2		1	1	1					1.4
Without blindfold		2	3		3	1	0					1.8
4. Champagne Pedestal												
With blindfold	3			8				3	7	3	3	4.5
Without blindfold	2			8				6	6	2	2	4.3
5. Breuer "Cesca"												
With blindfold	5			4				4	7	1	2	3.8
Without blindfold	4			3				4	7	4	3	4.1
6. "Prague"												
With blindfold	8			4				9	7	2	2	5.3
Without blindfold	8			4				6	8	3	3	5.3

TEST #2	Participants 1	2	3	4	5	6	7	8	9	10	11	Average
1. Eames Plywood	6	5	8	9	7	5	4	5	8	3	4	5.8
2. Shaker Ladderback Rocker	5	2	1	10	2	4	2	6	4	2	2	3.6
3. Windsor	5	5	3	7	3	4	3	9	3	1	4	4.2
4. Barcelona	5	7	7	7	5	5	3	6	8	7	6	6.0
5. Kagan "Cubo"	5	8	6	1	9	5	3	4	3	5	5	4.9
6. Wright Imperial Hotel	3	2	3	1	4	2	5	2	2	1	1	2.3
7. Breuer "Wassily"	5	3	3	5	8	4	6	5	4	4	3	4.5

Rating Scale: 1–10*

(The tests given at the Diffrient lecture have been shortened for clarification.)
*Chairs were rated on a rising scale, with 10 the highest possible score for beauty and comfort.

VIDEO TAPE: The other thing we did last week, which I announced just in passing when the session was over, was to videotape some of you as you were sitting. Now we want to replay the tapes in an effort to make your mind read what your body is telling you. On the tape are observed physical behavior patterns that provide reliable measures and honest criteria because they come directly from where it hurts. And so, the videotape, while still open to some interpretation, nevertheless presents an honest accounting of a chair. Let me first point out some of the cues that will enable you to read the language of the videotape. Notice the positions, the shifts, the crossing of arms and recrossing of legs. Take careful note of such as that man with the crossed leg; it relieves some under-leg pressure for him. The other fellow with his left leg crossed is using another chair for an arm rest. This guy has just the side of his back pressing against the top back part of the chair. Later on we'll see how annoying the top of that chair gets for him.

Now this section of film takes place after the break, after you had all been sitting for quite a while. We see a little more movement than in the earlier evening, when nobody moved very much. Now you see this man's back going back and forth. But this is still close to the beginning of the tape, so nobody is really uncomfortable yet. Now watch. He lifts himself up, pulls himself back, turns around, crosses a leg, and folds his arms, lacking anywhere else to put them. This sort of activity usually comes at points in the talk when there's a little humor or a break. At these times people feel they have a chance to shift. They are somehow reminded that they don't have to suffer.

Now watch this young lady for a while. Notice how she jerks forward and adjusts her back. Meanwhile, this other fellow keeps shifting his back also. Here we go . . . pick it up, move it back, and *s-t-r-a-i-g-h-t-e-n* the back, then hunch over—that's a correction from a slump.

This man is fidgeting in general, pressing back on that chair, hoping it will do better for him than it has so far, but it won't.

This young lady is really trying hard to get away from the back of that chair. Now, this shows the result of the slip-slide. The slip-slide is what you go into unconsciously when your muscles relax and aren't compensating for the lack of support in a chair. I shall break off this sequence when our young man picks up his lunch and starts to eat. . . .

Note again the crossing and recrossing of legs. It relieves underthigh pressure, usually. Other reasons for it, particularly prevalent with women with short legs, is to alternate the pressure under legs that are dangling. You just saw a little over three minutes of videotape and in that time one of you took at least three major wiggles. Others of you had to correct your slip-slide within that time also.

In the time between what I just showed you and what I'll be showing next, the same kinds of things continue to happen. As you learn to read the body better—that is, to read it as you would a textbook—you can choreograph these events as they are happening. You will automatically know, for instance, that when this fellow puts his hand between himself and the back of the chair it is because he's just *got* to relieve that back, so he's got his hand up there to make it comfortable. The chair is really not doing the job for him. And when you see someone like this lady in the black with her legs crossed, you will recognize that because she's not very tall she needs to do something with the pressure under her legs. And with this fellow leaning forward, he's probably tired of the back, too.

Anyway, I think you can see the point from this brief experiment—given a little bit more accuracy and better views of the entire body. If you can manage to have people watch something that is so vitally interesting that they are transported to another place in their heads, then, I assure you, you will get a good record of normal seating behavior. I can also assure you that there probably isn't one chair in a million on the market today with which that kind of feedback is ever taken before the chair is introduced into the market. I have no confirmation of this other than that there are not very many chairs that are very good. I can only conclude that no one ever tried them to any extent beforehand.

So then, the videotape is a useful tool in chair design for registering comfort.

SLIDES: The next thing we're going to do is look at some slides. I've accumulated some material out of our files that shows the background for our comfort assumptions. Then I will show the applications, in this case an airplane chair.

Sitting, as we learned last time, can be varied. For example, an overstuffed chair—big, soft, and fluffy. It represents almost everybody's idea of cloud-like comfort. The number of feathers in it gives the impression that it's going to be comfortable. In reality, in that big soft pile of down, your back sinks into a position that curves your spine in a backward—or convex—direction. Actually, we want the spine to take the slightly concave

The video tape system used to photograph the audience was manufactured by Panasonic. The camera was concealed, and only portions of the hour-long tape were eventually shown.

. . . you must pay attention and listen to your body. It is not as direct a feeling as pinching your fingers. Rather, it is like something going wrong in the basement of your house; you don't notice it right away. . . . In due time, your body begins to get a kind of inside ache. I can guarantee it.

contour on the right.

A big soft cushion chair totally wipes out any chance of that.

At the same time—depending on the softness of the cushion, how far you sink into the chair, your height, the length of your arms relative to your height, and a number of other factors —we must compensate. The arms are most likely to begin the necessary adjustments. I would guess that, if we had armchairs in this room, well over 50 percent of you would find your arms at the wrong height. But because no one is used to buying or using chairs that fit their arms, we compensate to the extent of putting strain on our shoulders. Remember in the videotape the number of persons that crossed their arms or put an arm on another chair? The strain from sitting in an improper arm position can, when the chair arms are too low, cause you to hunch after a while. On the other hand, the upward push against elbows and arms placed too high causes the shoulder to rise and you get the reverse kind of fatigue. There is a five-inch range among different people's elbow height. Yet I know of only one or two chairs commonly available that provide adjustable arms.

A common technical fact is that our tests have borne out that when the seat cushion as shown on the left comes up too far toward the back of your lower leg, it will put pressure on the bottom of your thigh. There happens to be a nerve that crosses under the thigh and over a bundle of muscles. If there is pressure on it over a period of time, it causes your foot and leg to go to sleep. So, as the diagram on the right shows, there should be some space there for clearance.

We didn't get into headrests yet, because we're going to discuss them with airplane chairs in a moment.

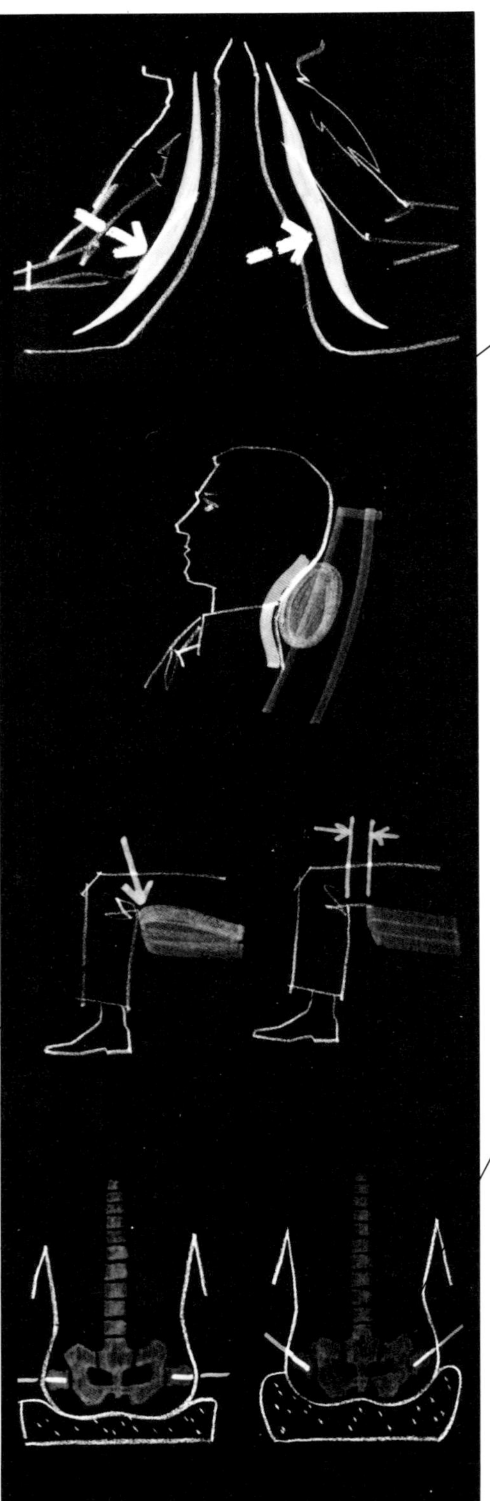

Let's note that when we talk about headrests we're really talking about a neck rest. You don't put something behind the point of your head to rest it on. That would be like trying to rest a marble on a hard surface; it's going to roll around. So the best place to put support is up under the skull to hold the skull up. That provides a far better rest than would something behind your head.

Again, of course, it must be an adjustable rest because bodies change height dramatically up toward the head. We find that they don't change dramatically in the distance from the seat up to the lumbar region of the spine, but they do from there up.

Another thing we found is that a seat cushion should allow you to sink into it only a given distance—usually about one and a half inches. If it gets above two inches, it's not very good, as you will find when you sit in a big soft easy chair like the one I just discussed. The reason is shown at the right, where you see the pelvic cage and the top of the upper leg bone, the femur. The femur plugs into the pelvic cage in a little right-angle kink and when you get pressure bearing up from the cushion, the point of the bone tends to roll upward, causing a great deal of tension and discomfort.

But now you must pay attention and listen to your body. It is not as direct a feeling as pinching your fingers. Rather, it is like something going wrong in the basement of your house; you don't notice it right away. It takes a while to notice the leaky pipe or the clogged drain. In due time, your body begins to get a kind of inside ache. I can guarantee it. You can't quite put your finger on it; in truth you couldn't, because it's way in there where the bones are connected.

I shall throw this in as a clue to tell a story. After a long time of studying

"Human beings must group, sit or recline, confound them, . . . I have been black and blue in some spot, somewhere, almost all my life from too intimate contact with my own early furniture. . . . Human use and comfort should not be taxed to pay dividends on any designer's idiosyncrasy."
—Frank Lloyd Wright, *Autobiography, Horizon Press,* New York, 1976.

He (Feldenkrais) simply says that unless you sit perfectly upright and stack all your vertebrae perfectly straight, which most of us can't do anyway, then you have no chance whatsoever of sitting down without harming yourself.

Some people can sit a remarkably long time. I notice people in offices who sit in a chair in the morning, don't get up until lunch, come in and sit down in the afternoon again, and don't get up. In fact, they tend to ring the buzzer for anything they need. They're executives.

and working on chairs that I thought achieved a respectable degree of comfort, I had a visitor. His name was Moshe Feldenkrais. He had written a book on body awareness, *Awareness Through Movement,* and he came in and he listened to me go through my talk much as I'm giving it to you now. Finally I turned to him and asked, "What do you think?" And he told me that nobody should ever lean back in a reclining chair.

He went on to present another whole principle of comfort, one that would be in total disagreement with practically all the experts I've come in contact with. He simply says that unless you sit perfectly upright and stack all your vertebrae perfectly straight, which most of us can't do anyway, then you have no chance whatsoever of sitting down without harming yourself. His basic principle is that you must never use a backrest. Of course you must take his course to learn how to sit this way.

This is a set of x-rays we took a long time ago. They have been touched up to bring out more clearly the area we've been talking about that gives us the most back trouble. The lower five segments are the lumbar segments. Eighty percent of the motion of the back from the neck down is taken up by these five segments. The next twelve are the thoracic and they each connect to the rib cage. There's not a lot of movement in the thoracic section, but there is enough to enable the upper part of your body to collapse to a degree that can be uncomfortable. And there's enough movement also to allow the muscles to stretch in the other direction. But the bulk of the flexibility and movement in the back comes from the lumbar section as well as the neck, or cervical area.

A funny thing happens when you sit down. The bottom spinal segment tends to rotate in such a way that it permits of yet another curve.

Now notice where the chair ends; the seat ends at the lower leg. There's no pressure up under the nerve section of the thigh. There was a diaphragm made of a harder piece of material inserted in this deep cushion to keep the person from sinking too far into it. I don't think the person is sinking more than an inch and three quarters to two inches, maximum. This forms a basic reference document for us. It's like a blueprint.

We also looked at the way the neck bends in the cervical section; the seven cervical spinal segments are shown here. As you can see, there's a great deal of flex here. This has everything to do with our studies regarding support of the neck. We have never been able to solve the cervical support problem for aircraft chairs, by the way, because the adjustable parts on airplane chairs have a way of consistently breaking down.

This is the chair we used. The body x-ray was taken in segments. This is an average-size male, and his arms are on that pillow simply to get them out of the way of the image. The chair, as you can see, is on a dolly; it rolls back and forth, up and down in front of the x-ray machine. In that way we get a mosaic of his entire body, forming a basic reference.

Other basic references we use are the variation in body sizes. Here we see a dimension comparison (next page) between the smallest female in our data file, whom we call the "2½-percentile female," and the "97½-percentile male." Notice the difference in height. It's almost inconceivable that the same chair could work for both people; yet they will

Photographs and illustrations provided through the courtesy of Niels Diffrient, Henry Dreyfuss Associates.

Look at three body types—the ectomorph, endomorph, and mesomorph. How could one chair possibly suit all three?

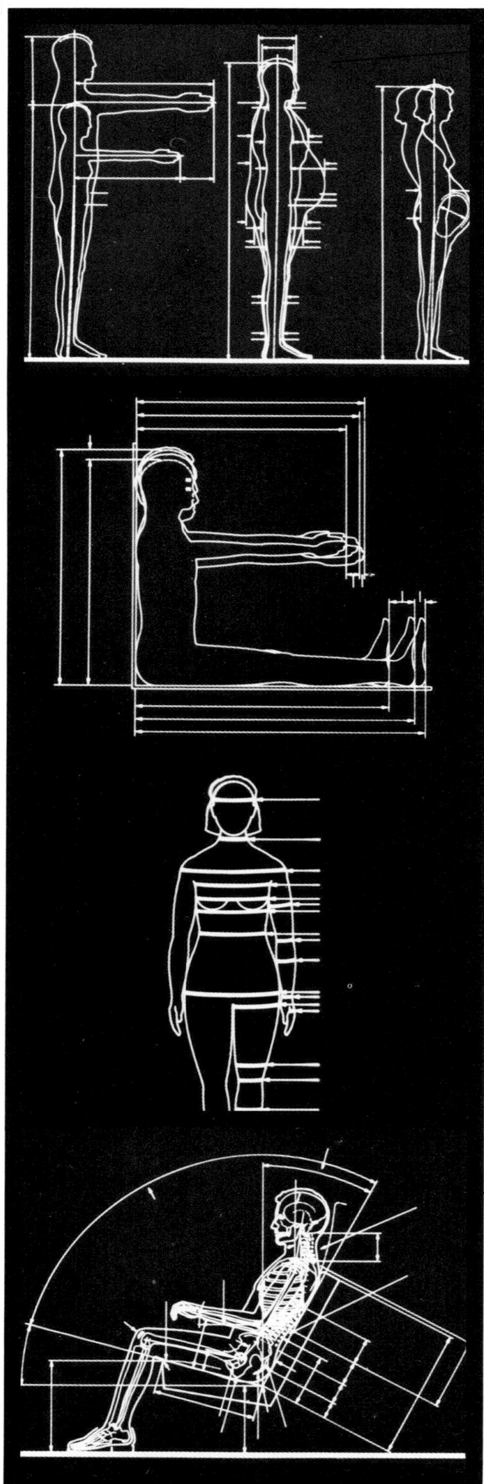

seldom have much choice.

Look at three body types—the ectomorph, endomorph, and mesomorph. How could one chair possibly suit all three? And of course rarely taken into account is the pregnant woman. Her whole system of balance is different, whether she is sitting or standing. She has to compensate in every position for the weight of the child.

Other seldom-considered differences among people are ethnic proportions. Let us consider first an Oriental. He may have the same length of torso as I have, but traditionally, his legs are shorter than mine. I'm a Caucasian of about average height. An Oriental with a comparable-length torso might stand over an inch shorter than I. The difference is entirely in the length of his legs. A chair that is comfortable for him has to be quite different in proportion than one comfortable for me.

On the other hand, blacks tend to have very long legs and a shorter torso—a different ratio altogether.

Then we have all kinds of armlength variations. Again the Oriental is supposed to have a shorter arm than a Caucasian, and the black, longer. Three different armrests are called for.

This shows the diameter of all the parts of the body. As you see, the variations are considerable.

The center of gravity of our various parts is useful to study when figuring out the density of cushioning. It is a study that's rarely done. One last thing that can have a very considerable effect on seating comfort is the amount of clothing worn. Some clothing adds up to two inches of bulk around the outside of the body. When working out a design for a chair in a crawler/tractor that's to be used out in the cold, we must consider the fact that people with a lot of additional bulk from clothing will require support and freedom of movement from the chair. We must revise the entire chair geometry for special cases like these.

This last diagram relates back to the x-rays you saw. It shows the spine in more or less the same curve that we were able to record in the x-ray, indicating a lounge chair posture. Notice how much more open than 90 degrees the back angle is. Actually, 90 degrees would be about 20 degrees forward of this, as indicated by the drawn-in arc. Our reference is taken from the two lines you see drawn in on the diagram. The seat reference point is where the two come together. Those two lines are about the only reference lines we've been able to find on the side that are consistently useful for measuring the position of the body.

Now that we have a set of data, what do we do? We want to make a real three-dimensional chair that conforms to the data. We have the proper contour of the body, the doctor has assured us; and we know where the spine should be on an x-ray. But when you sit somebody down on a cushioned chair, how do you know you've got the body where the diagrams indicated it should be? That was a problem we had to solve, so we decided we had to go all the way and really find out. We built the machine shown at the right here with a 60-percentile man sitting in it.

It has adjustable arms, both for angle and height. The seat height—effective height—can be adjusted simply by moving a board up and down to raise the foot position. The angle of the back can be changed as well. In addition, the entire contour that supports the cushion can be changed. I'll get to that in a moment.

These diagrams are from the publication Henry Dreyfuss Associates prepared, called *Humanscale 1/2/3,* available from MIT Press.

"Robert Ardrey, Edward T. Hall, Konrad Lorenz and many others have demonstrated how in shaping our surroundings we set up a closed feedback loop that ultimately shapes us."—Victor Papanek, "Revolution, Social Change and Design," *Environment/Planning and Design,* Summer 1971.

... if you sit in a chair and the back isn't comfortable, you drastically begin to slide down. You don't notice it, but it happens. Then you get to the point where you're caving in. Now the frequency of those slides and the number of minutes one takes from beginning to end are important indicators of seat comfort.

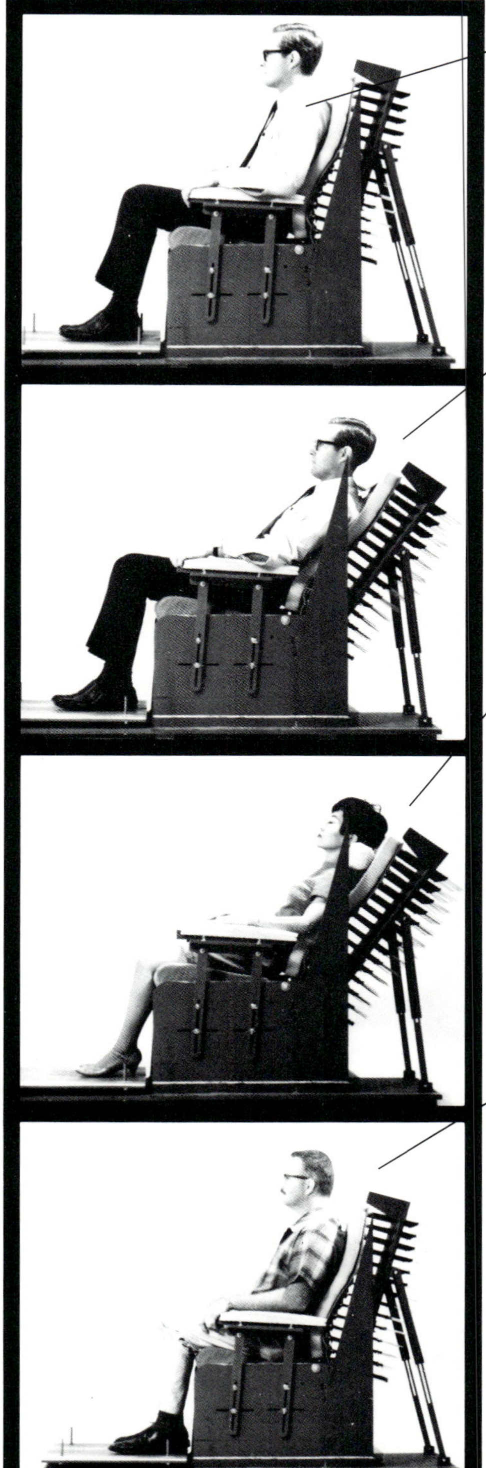

Here it is in an upright position. It was done for an aircraft chair design, so it reclines.

And here it is in reclining position. Notice we use the skull support type of cushion for head support.

So much for the 60-percentile male. Let's now look at the same setting but with a 3- or 4-percentile female seated in it. We are getting her feet to touch the ground, which is more than a lot of chairs can do. She has her leg right up against the cushion, which is not so good, and I'll explain why it has to be that way. She has some lumbar support but not where she should have it, because, as an Oriental, she has a torso longer than the torso of the Caucasian woman of the same height we've worked with. Her recline posture is all right and the arms are reasonably good. There's validity in designing nonadjustable arms if there is some width to play with, because if the chair arms are too high, you just have to make them wide enough so that the elbows can move outward as they are forced to rest at a higher than natural position.

Let's consider the cushion. Look at this larger man. He happens to have a very long torso and short legs, but he does have air space behind the knees. He sits slightly forward, without being too far forward. It is important that a chair cushion be long enough to keep the tall person feeling secure. If it is too short, he will feel as though he's falling off the front of the chair. Conversely, the short person with this long cushion will feel the pressure on the back of his legs.

The purpose of this chair was that we were trying to get measurements of all these different sizes and weights of people as their bodies came to rest within the thickness of the cushion. We knew the shape we wanted the person's backside to have, and we wanted to find out if we were getting it within the cushion. So the back of our test chair actually looked like this. Those protrusions are tubes, and in each is a shaft. These pass through the cushion to the front. You can see some of them sticking out. They are knitting needles.

Each of the discs you see here supports a section of the body. By turning the threaded shafts, we could change the position of any one of the discs, thereby giving as an x/y/z coordinate system of contour change

on the back side of the chair. We can also adapt it to three dimensions to get any shape we want.

In this schematic diagram the foam padding is shaded. Note the outline of the round disc we saw before and the hollow shaft with the back support posts. This is one of the knitting nee-

Daniel Tobin, D.D.S. asks: "Whose mind or psyche do we wittingly or unwittingly tend to overlook? . . . the patient's state of mind and all which that connotes, may be neglected from the onset in our quest for technical achievement . . . from the Foreword, Martin Protell. *Psychodynamics in Dental Practice.* Chas. C. Thomas, Springfield, Illinois.

It would be easy to design a comfortable airplane chair if space were not a primary concern. Airlines are economically feasible only when the optimum numbers of passengers can be transported. . . . In effect, it is not within the seating designer's prerogative to consider passenger comfort alone, ideal as that would be. Airline seating is always a compromise. . . .

dles going through. When someone sat down on the cushion and depressed it to a given contour, the knitting needles were pushed back, thereby changing the position of the points of the knitting needles where they stuck out through the back of the chair. If you will recall the x-ray, it was important for us to record that contour of the body and to learn what the related spine contour would be. Once we knew this curve, we knew if we were receiving the kind of comfort we wanted in the chair.

We did the same thing for the seat. The needles were turned around with the points up and we simply pushed until we got a response from above. Sort of hazardous, this business.

In another test we took heavy aluminum foil and painted black grid marks on it. Then we let people sit on the aluminum foil. By carefully sitting them down, then standing them up again, we got a very cheap kind of cast in the shape of the body. And that could indicate too much pressure on any given point and would confirm the kind of information we were getting from the knitting needles.

Several dozen subjects of all sizes eventually provided us with a great many data. This was converted again to drawings showing the range of cushion depression according to size and weight of the individual. Every individual body differed.

Now just for comparison, this is an existing airplane chair. The short woman we saw before is seated in it. The chair is digging into the back of her leg. Notice also how her elbow is off the armrest. How can that be? Don't forget she has a long torso and short legs and quite short arms. This just serves to point up again all the variances we must take into account.

This is the same chair, several actually finished. They have some features that work quite interestingly. Keep in mind that there is very little room in an airplane, so the chair ultimately doesn't have much room either. This is a first-class chair. It provides more space than most of us use when flying. The arms are generous and they are farther apart than in ordinary airplane seats. I can point out the contour developed for the lumbar area far better on this chair because it is so wide. One of the few adjustments that we were able to get into this chair is an air bag in the lumbar region so that the passenger can change the contour of the lower back. Unfortunately, it doesn't show in the model. It is adjusted by a separate button: a round button will recline the chair and the square one will adjust the lower back. The amount of change obtainable was within the range of acceptability for anybody. In other words, the adjustment couldn't hurt anybody's back. It was designed simply for two things—to adapt to a person's particular form and to make it possible for him to change the shape of the back once in a while, just for the sake of change. The sad thing is that people generally don't perceive that this does them good and didn't bother to learn how to use the adjustment, so in time the airlines figured that it wasn't selling more tickets and abandoned it. It is, nevertheless, a very valuable device and I'm sure it will come back someday.

As any of you who have flown know, when the person in front of you reclines, he reclines right back into your lap. We designed this chair so that only the upper part of the chair reclines. The lower part changes too, but not in a way that moves backward into another passenger.

Again in consideration for the per-

Airlines generally try to trick you into thinking you're getting a big reclinable chair by putting the upright position of the chair *very* upright, quite uncomfortably upright.

son behind, the tables for the chair come out of the center console and not from the back of the chair ahead.

Other little incidentals about our airplane chair were its own separate foot space and leg space and an angled floor board element to provide a better foot rest.

Now let's look at the side view of the chair for another view of the way the back reclines. Again, these chairs, although they are designed to look large and luxurious, have a very shallow fore-aft depth because the seating allowance per person is only 36 to 38 inches in most airplanes, and as close as 34 inches on the cheapie overseas flights. Imagine bodies floating in space every 34 inches! The only way to get any space at all in front is to use a very thin chair because, obviously, the thicker the chair, the less room you've got. The body space is preordained.

Now, this slide shows where the upper back goes as it is moved back and forth. Nothing changes down below. The movement is kept at a minimum so that it doesn't interfere with the comfort of others.

Now, this is the tourist section chair, similar in many respects to the other, but notice how much thinner it gets. In this case there is no room on the side to hold a table, so it goes on the back ahead.

Again, here is the recline. Of course you haven't paid as much money as in first class, so you don't get much recline. But there's a big difference, and it's psychological, I suppose, as much as anything. Some airlines try to trick you into thinking you're getting a large recline movement by putting the upright position of the chair *very* upright, uncomfortably upright. And of course there's now a law forbidding you to recline the back until you've gotten into the air and the seat belt sign is off. We think that the upright chair trick is fairly stupid: why not put these chairs in upright position at a comfortable angle in the first place? If you must sit upright all those minutes waiting for the sign to change before you may recline, at least you'd be comfortable.

I mentioned earlier that we have never solved the head-support problem. We've tried everything but have never yet been able to improve on a loose pillow. Figuring out an effective way to provide head support, at very minimum cost, when the head support has to move eight, nine inches up and down (that's the range of head support from the smallest to the largest person) has eluded us.

Other considerations that I think are important in designing a thing like the airline chair include attention to details. For example, the passenger should not have to risk skinning his knuckles while adjusting the tray table unit, so we pad the back of the tourist chair.

These chairs are designed specifically for a 727, which is not a large-sized jet. I think for that size of airplane, these are the best airline chairs.

It would be easy to design a comfortable airplane chair if space were not a primary concern. Airlines are economically feasible only when the optimum numbers of passengers can be transported from one place to another. In effect, it is not within the seating designer's prerogative to consider passenger comfort alone, ideal as that would be. Airliner seating is always a compromise, and to my way of thinking, the more information on hand about the dynamics of human comfort, the better will be the compromise.

The main purpose of this sequence was to bring out the fact that the in-

"More than one civilization has seriously tried to reduce the human physique to a statistical norm. The Egyptians, Greeks, Romans and Renaissance Europeans tried, . . . Nicholas Andry de Boisregard, [in his] *L'Orthopedie* of 1741 . . . set forth the basic anthropometric measurements for designing chairs."—Roger Yee, "Slouching Towards Barcelona", *Progressive Architecture,* February 1975.

. . . we distributed some literature on the chair. Generally, nobody ever bothered to read it. Most people don't even read how to get out of the airplane in case it crashes, much less how to be comfortable in the chair.

. . . no product ever gets much better if the consumers don't express their distaste for it. Airline people are not about to tell you their chairs are bad, nor will anybody else . . . you wait to see how many people complain . . . So, I will advise you: if things annoy you . . . make it known.

tegration of technical information on comfort with the design of the form is possible without sacrifice to the attractive quality of the form. I mean that those of you who design don't really want to bring out an unattractive product and have to use the excuse, "Well, it's terribly comfortable." This is the reverse of the design concept apparent in many of the chairs we sat in before, which were terribly good-looking though quite uncomfortable.

So, what I tried to illustrate through the slides is that if you know in some depth the limitations of the notion of comfort, it is possible to design good-looking chairs that are comfortable.

Question: How long can a person sit in a chair?
Diffrient: Some people can sit a remarkably long time. I notice people in offices who sit in a chair in the morning, don't get up until lunch, come in and sit down in the afternoon again, and don't get up. In fact, they tend to ring the buzzer for anything they need. They're executives. I make a point of getting up every time I want something from somebody instead of ringing the buzzer. At least I get up and walk around a little bit. The thing about the airplane of course is that you do get trapped, and you accept it, but you compensate by wiggling.

Remember the things I told you we looked for in order to read the videotapes properly. A classic is what we call the "slow slide." For example, if you sit in a chair and the back isn't comfortable, you generally begin to slide down. You don't notice it, but it happens. Then you get to the point where you're caving in. Now the frequency of those slides and the number of minutes one takes from beginning to end are important indicators of seat comfort. Another thing we look for, of course, is the crossing of the legs, which we videotaped here last week. You can time the process of crossing and recrossing the legs in individuals and get some clue to how much pressure is being applied under the thighs.

Question: What's the difference between a truck driver's seat and an automobile seat?
Diffrient: Well, a truck driver's seat is much more upright. The legs are closer and hang straight down. By the time you sink down into most automobile seats you are no more than four or five inches off the floor of the car. Then the other thing of course about automobile chairs now is that the manufacturers and dealers sell you on the pretense of comfort of the bucket seat which has flanges up on either side of the seat, and of course a flange on the back too. These parts of the cushion tend to give it the bucket look and will sell you visually on being comfortable, but they're the worst things in the world because they do what the diagram showed in the film: they roll the upper joint of the femur against the socket edge. You find yourself squirming in your bucket seat and that's the reason for it.

Question: Please explain what you meant by compensating for body support in a chair.
Diffrient: Well, when you sit on a stool, you pretty much have to sit at a right angle. You can lean forward; you brace yourself a bit. At any other angle you use muscles to support the cantilever of your upper back. In other words, it's like balancing. If you balance your spine from the top of your pelvic cage, you don't need much muscle power to do it, but if it gets out of balance, you've got to use your muscles to keep it up there.

Question: How is it that the airlines haven't done something more positive about the comfort of passengers?
Diffrient: The thing you find is that no product ever gets much better if the consumers don't express their distaste for it. Airline people are not about to tell you their chairs are bad, nor will anybody else. It happens to be easier to get rid of some comfort devices on an airline chair than to maintain them. Then you wait to see how many people complain. If it's a nominal number, the airline doesn't put them back on and so saves money. So, I will advise you: If things annoy you, not just in airline chairs but anything, make it known.

Question: The other thing is, Americans are very hard on anything that can be moved; they yank and jam——
Diffrient: Why, they want to get rid of them, I guess——

Question: ——and they don't ask how things are supposed to be used and they don't read diagrams.
Diffrient: No, I know that for a fact because we distributed some literature on the chair. Generally, nobody ever bothered to read it. Most people don't even read how to get out of the airplane in case it crashes, much less how to be comfortable in the chair.

Question: Is it possible to get a lumbar adjustment for American house chairs, lounge chairs?
Diffrient: Not that I know of. You can adjust the lumbar in Volvo automobiles and John Deere Tractors and some specialized vehicle seats. To my knowledge I've never seen a chair, household chair, where there's been a conscious effort to make a lumbar adjustment. There are few adjustments on household furniture.

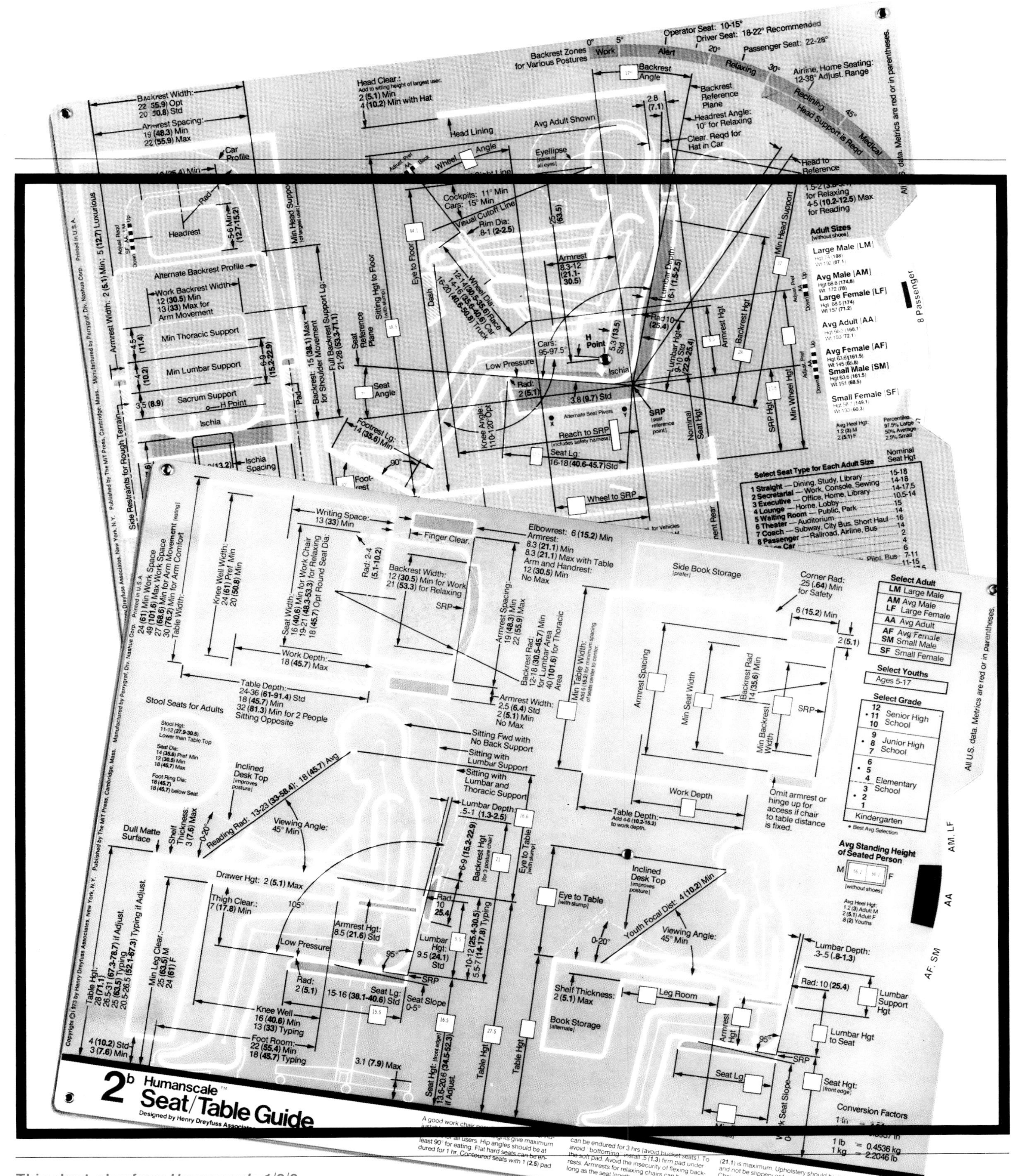

This chart, also from *Humanscale 1/2/3* (MIT Press), adjusts by turning the dial to different kinds of chairs (theatre chair, secretarial chair, passenger car chair, race car seat, etc.) and the appropriate information appears related to them.

Blade

Mary Plumb Blade, born in Salt Lake City in 1913, is Professor of Mechnical Engineering and Dean of Engineering, Cooper Union, holds a degree in electrical engineering from the University of Utah, an M.S. in Industrial Engineering from Columbia, and has studied at MIT and Yale. She has done a great deal of work in Kinematics (the study of moving parts), and her design approach considers the inescapable principles of mechanics. "Most things don't work because these principles are not applied," she says. "Such things as the force of gravity and the acceleration of the human body cannot be ignored." She is presently carrying on research on the physiological effects of inactivity and weightlessness.

. . . if you don't use muscles, you don't supply them with fresh blood; and without exercise, they start to atrophy immediately. If your leg is in a cast, the leg shrinks in size from nonuse. If you sit quietly in a chair for too long, you may damage yourself physically.

It is the force of gravity, or the attraction of the Earth, . . . which keeps us sitting in our chairs and not floating in space; the force that pulls us down on a chair and pulls the chair to the floor is also pulling every person toward every other person. Think of it for a moment!

Tonight I'm going to tell you about the dynamics of people. Some chairs are very handsome as structures but may fail as a proper place to sit. Tonight I'd like to tell you about the relationship of a chairman, chairwoman, or chairperson to the chair.

You can't sit in a chair comfortably for very long. For example, everyone has had the experience of sitting in an automobile too long; truck drivers, who sit the longest in vehicles, have made a rule that they will sit only for five hours, and even that is debilitating. Lying in bed is also debilitating. The interesting thing is that if you don't use muscles, you don't supply them with fresh blood; and without exercise, they start to atrophy immediately. If your leg is in a cast, the leg shrinks in size from nonuse. If you sit quietly in a chair for too long, you may damage yourself physically.

As humans have evolved, we have managed to develop without chairs attached to our behinds. Therefore, we must study the dynamic relationship between the chair and the sitter in our present culture.

We in Western culture have increasingly become accustomed both to restricting our emotions and being required to sit for long periods. In the East, the Japanese used to sit on their own legs. They don't do this very much anymore, because when they go to school, factories, or offices, they mimic their Western neighbors. Now they're sitting in chairs, and many have lost the ability to sit on their legs. They are as uncomfortable and as pained as we are when we visit their teahouses.

The first most comfortable position is something that I would like to call a "float." The float provides utmost freedom to move. If we were to release our earthly bonds to be freer than birds, we would have six degrees of freedom.

To describe our motion, set up three directions, down (or up), right (or left), and forward (or back). We can glide or translate in these three directions at any moment. We can also turn clockwise (or counterclockwise) in these three directions. Thus at any moment the most freedom to move can be described as a combination of these six motions—three glides and three rotations. This is the motion we might experience at sea or in a small airplane.

Because the body is a collection of linked parts (legs, toes, arms, fingers, head, ears, etc.), the motion of any part relative to the rest of the body is partially constrained or limited. Thus if we want to throw our legs around, we can't throw them very far. Also, we can't escape from standing on the earth; we're stuck. If you try to jump off, you can't jump very far. If you're going to design a structure that will hold you up off the earth, you will have to consider the relationship of the center of gravity of the earth to the structure's center of gravity and to your own.

We can't float, because of gravity. The free body is a myth which belongs only in outer space or in physics class. This is because of that mysterious and not understood phenomenon that causes our bodies to stick to or be attracted to larger bodies. The larger the bodies and the closer they are to one another, the more they attract one another and gravitate toward one another. Thus, your body sticks to the chair and the chair sticks to the floor.

The force of gravity, which is a measure of this attraction, is a universal and most important consideration in the dynamics of shape. It is the force of gravity, or the attraction of the Earth (a heavy body close to us), which keeps us sitting in our chairs and not floating in space; the force that pulls us down on a chair and pulls the chair to the floor is also pulling every person toward every other person.

If one were in a fetal or roughly spherical position, the gravitational force could be represented as a vector acting on a line through a central point of the body, directed to the center of the Earth, representing the magnitude of the force by which the Earth is attracting our body.

If one were floating near the Earth, the force would be pulling us downward. The bird, for example, though free to move in space, is continually pulled toward the Earth and either pushes against the fluid air by flapping its wings or is pushed upward by the force of the moving air. Only the angels

"A chair could be defined as a device which contains a somewhat erect body and holds it from being pulled to the earth."—Blade

No one in this room will stay still for very long. You'll cross your legs; you'll put your head on your arm; you'll cross your arms. If you're trying to be a little more comfortable in that seat, you're going to move.

or outer space astronauts can therefore truly float.

By moving an arm, squirming, turning, or shifting our position, we exert not only a gravitational force but also a dynamic force caused either by exerting a muscle action or by letting some part of ourselves fall.

Everyone has had the jarring experience of falling a few inches, as when one "falls" down an unnoticed curb. If you see the curb and carefully (though swiftly) walk down using heel and toe, there is no sudden jarring. You have subconsciously used a sort of springing action to minimize impact. If you let yourself fall face down, your head hits the ground in about half a second, at about 15 miles per hour.

If you drop into a chair you are suddenly loading it with at least twice your weight.

When the mind—or spirit—is fully occupied, the body seems to be tranquilized. Usually, however, when sitting, we fling ourselves about, with feet on the ground, arms spread on the back and arms of a chair or nearby table. With torso and buttocks we also distribute the earth's pull on our bodies to various parts of the chair, the floor, table, wall, bench, bed, or whatever we touch nearby.

As soon as there is a pause in conversation, we slump and change position. No one in this room will stay still for very long. You'll cross your legs; you'll put your head on your arm; you'll cross your arms. If you're trying to be a little more comfortable in that seat, you're going to move.

The designer Niels Diffrient, who has been analyzing chairs and their comfortability, observing and testing many people in many chairs, has told me that *chairs are uncomfortable.* Most people when questioned say they have never found a comfortable chair. Mr. Diffrient has made many anatomical and esthetic studies of chairs designed for long hours of sitting (for airplane travel). The results are chairs that can be adjusted to fit a particular person's back and his body type.

Again, my thesis is that sitters should move. Long constraint damages a person progressively. We should move our muscles.

Chair designers design empty chairs. Looking at advertisements for chairs and the interiors illustrated in magazines, we might assume no one sits down. The chairs are empty, structures to be admired for their visual properties. Some are handsome architecture like the Barcelona chair, and some are deeply upholstered bastions and stuffed fortresses. As an example, we can see the empty chairs in a Sunday newspaper. There are about a hundred chairs. None is occupied, and the designs are visual abstractions that are

Again, my thesis is that sitters should move. Long constraint damages a person progressively. We should move our muscles.

NASA studies reveal the effect of weightlessness on human bodies which have been in space up to 89 days. The data shows that Soviet astronauts do not suffer decalcification (loss of the mass and density of the bones) to the extent that the Americans do, perhaps because of the emphasis on exercise in the Russian daily regimen.

read without the dynamic reality that comes from a person *in* and *on* a chair.

I would like to see advertisements of chairs with people in at least some of them. This might attract persons to better and more comfortable chairs and would illustrate the poor design qualities of those chairs that are mismatched to the dynamics of the seated person.

Let us fill the empty chair. Let us see the total shape, chair plus person, chairman, or chairwoman, and study the dynamics of the total system.

Chairs may be classified by their design in four ways—Stabiles, Incipient Unstabiles, Unstabiles, and Mobiles.

STABILES are chairs that are designed to be stable. Usually heavy, large, and armed, they have a geometry which ensures a low center of gravity. Typical Stabiles are traditional thrones, from which it would be difficult to be overthrown or upset. Equipped with a seat belt, they would be even more secure for the occupant. Some of the very heavy living-room and men's-club chairs are closely related to thrones.

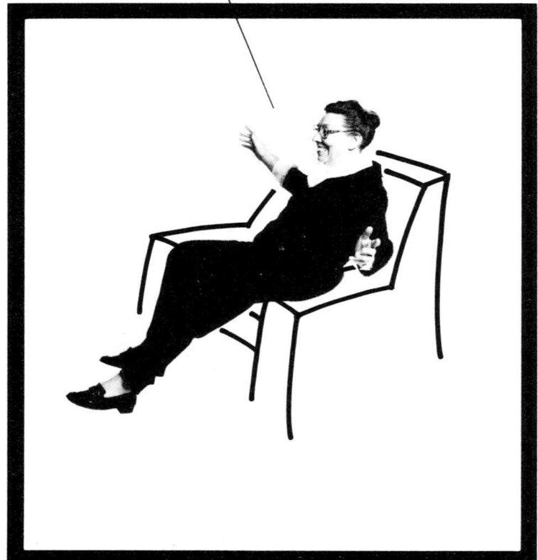

The Stabiles cannot move regardless of the movement of the occupant. Though it would be unlikely that a queen or king would throw her or his legs over the arms or back of a throne, it is not unusual for a commoner to do so. The point is that the Stabile remains unmoved.

The Stabile has no dynamic properties, but it allows the freedom to move, roll, and spring out. It does not interact.

Less monumental but also a Stabile is a bench. This seems to be the usual "chair" occupied by the Virgin Mary as depicted by artists of the Middle Ages. The bench is usually covered by her voluminous clothes. She can move about on the bench.

The bench as a structure is no more stable, intrinsically, than a chair. If the occupant is not seated on it squarely, the bench usually becomes an edge. Therefore it cannot be classified as an Incipient Unstabile.

INCIPIENT UNSTABILES are designed to be rigid structures, but they are light enough to be moved. Stability is regained when the occupant leans the chair back against a wall or steadies the chair with the feet. Teetering, or incipient unstability, is achieved sometimes by rocking. When the back of the chair touches the wall, the position creates a temporary bucket seat, which is relatively stable if the occupant stretches his/her feet out and upward on a desk in front of the chair.

It has been said that the natural administrative capability of a

"If we seat a person in a 'fitted' seat so that the person may be inactive for hours at a time (for example in an automobile, airplane, theatre, or viewing TV) we are improperly seating the person. The person may suffer bone demineralization and calcium loss, and with extended inactivity, osteoporosis."—Blade.

Chair designers design empty chairs. Looking at advertisements for chairs and the interiors illustrated in magazines, we might assume no one sits down. The chairs are empty, structures to be admired for their visual properties.

When a person sits down, he applies the exact same force on the chair's seat as the seat applies on him, for two reasons—first: The force of an object is equal to its mass times its acceleration to the earth (32 ft/sec^2)—second: Newton's Third Law of Motion states, "To every action there is an equal and opposite reaction". . . . When this concept is applied to the seat, the force the seat applies to the person is equal and opposite to the force your body applies to the seat.

Yesterday on the front page of *The New York Times* there was a picture of nine important judges in New York. They were all sitting at a round table and they had the most wonderful, well-designed, comfortable, stuffed chairs you ever saw. And every one of them was sitting on the edge.

person can be seen if he feels comfortable with his feet up on a desk. (We have to train women to feel comfortable in such a position—and thereby develop their natural abilities for administrative work!)

Instability is *incipient while* the occupant is returning to the intended, stable position. As the person rises, he/she may go over backward or have some other catastrophe or the chair may suffer failure and slip or break. It's a popular form of musical chairs.

UNSTABILES may give the appearance of a stable structure but become unstable when there is a poor match between chair and occupant. If there is a marked disparity between them, there will be a dynamic interaction, with the occupant toppling over or being forced by the geometry of the chair to grapple with it to remain seated at all.

Now, I'm going to talk about my favorite chair. This is what I call the "edge" and I would like to see all the architects here and all designers of chairs and all the people who think seriously about their buttocks design edges, because I really think this is the chair of the future. The person who achieves stability in this way has a three-point stable contact—edge contact with the buttocks, and two feet spread apart on the ground. This is a stable position yet even leaves the person free to squirm occasionally. Yesterday on the front page of *The New York Times* there was a picture of nine important judges in New York. They were all sitting at a round table and they had the most wonderful, well-designed,

comfortable, stuffed chairs you ever saw. And every one of them was sitting on the edge. So I think that what you ought to do, if you want to design chairs for people who are gesturing, conversing, talking, trying to persuade people, judging, or doing arts, is design a chair with a nice, usable edge, because you'll find these people on the edge anyway.

Here's yet another edge. People, how many hours can you sit at a bar? I don't know. Some people

say a lot; I think a long time. So, here is a bar. The bar is down here at your feet. When you move suddenly, unbalancing the chair that serves as an edge, the edge becomes incipiently unstable.

A bar is a good place to work. When we talk about sitting at a bar, it's two bars actually, the one at the foot and another at the arms. Recently I talked to a well-known designer who does a lot of his work in a photography laboratory and who had a big problem there. He employed several people in the darkroom and he wanted to know how you can make a darkroom laboratory comfortable. He built a

"People gesture, converse, try to persuade, judge, do arts, or whatever when they are sitting. So design a chair with a nice, usable *edge*, because you'll find these people sitting on the edge anyway."—Blade.

bar for his employees to work at, and found this to be a comfortable position for them. Then there was the man who tried to solve the problem of absenteeism in his factory. He employed women who did delicate work all day at a table. Each of them suffered from backache and stayed out a lot, so he designed a chair that would fit their work. Since they had to lean forward he installed a bar, and after a while, the absenteeism decreased. This was on the order of the Hawthorne effect, which you've probably heard of. You know, management does something and employees respond by changing their performance. Then, after a while, the absenteeism or other old ways will resume.

In a contemporary version of David's "Mlle. Charlotte du Val d'Ognes" (from an advertisement for a bucket chair) the girl is seated on the edge, painting. It is virtually impossible to sit very long on the edge of a bucket, let alone to paint.

The problem with buckets is that once you get into one, you can get stuck and can't get out.

MOBILES are chairs designed for motion. They may be Rockers, Springs, Swings, Hammocks, Swivels, and Rollers. Sufficient constraint is required so that the occupant stays with the mobile chair and the force of motion does not move the chair-occupant system beyond a dynamic equilibrium, or beyond the elastic limit of the system.

The rockers of the rocking chair are not parallel but toed-in at the rear. This geometry prevents the rocker from traveling over the floor and from rocking too far backward and overturning.

Spring chairs are designed to vibrate the occupant but may eject

him/her. Swings and Hammocks require the occupant to learn how to develop uneven rhythms to create a Coriolis force, which enables him to oscillate merely by moving some part of the body to raise and lower his center of gravity.

The Experimental Environmental Laboratory (EEL) in Boston designed a swinging table and benches attached as a unit in circular form. Half a dozen people could sit around the table. Every time anyone made the slightest motion, the table and whole ensemble would move. They were engaged in a group project, and each person was always sensitive to what everyone else was doing.

It was also the EEL that cut an automobile body in two and used the rear half with upholstered seat and canopied top to make a small cavern for seating two in a living room. This double chair had a sheltered, isolated feeling and made intimate conversations possible. It retains a shell-like audio property and an unusual "chair environment" for a living room.

We have progressed from Stabiles to Unstabiles, thence to Mobiles. Now consider the ultimate mobile.

The milking stool is one-legged. The milker has three degrees of freedom to rotate about the single pointed leg, with spread feet on the ground and buttocks on the seat, giving dynamic stability. The stool is attached to the milker by a strap, ready for use with the next cow. Later "improvements" gave

"The Hawthorne Tests, conducted at the Western Electric Company . . . 1927 to 1932, tried to determine the best working conditions by improving different variables in a worker's environment such as relief from fatigue (and) monotony, increased wage incentive, and changes in methods of su pervision."— Carl Heyel, *The Encyclopedia of Management,* Van Nostrand Reinhold.

I one time sat on a steep mountain cliff for several days. When rescued, I couldn't stand up. Many others have told of a similar physical disability after sitting—for a short time even—in deeply stuffed chairs.

the milking stool another two to three legs, thereby restricting the rotational movement of the milkmaid. The original milking stool was the basis for the modern swivel chair. If you would like to have one in your living room, you should first bolt a socket to the floor to hold the sharp point. Your stool will then pivot from this point.

The minimum seat is the bicycle seat. It is a precarious perch, but the dynamics of the moving bicycle and the skilled motions of the cyclist who is attached to pedals and handlebars (sometimes not to handle bars) makes the bicycle seat dynamically stabile. (It is virtually impossible to make a bike unridable by a skilled rider.) The seat or saddle, which can hardly be called a chair, gives the rider the maximum freedom for rotating and stretching the legs, bending the torso, and pulling on the handlebars to exert more force through the legs to the pedals, thence to the wheels.

A bicycle seat or saddle is a spring-loaded pivot point for a dynamic, moving occupant.

In looking for chairs that retain their capability of motion with the sitter, their simplicity, economic use of material and style, and their portability, we might look at Eva Zeisel's chair design of 1949.

The structure is a continuous tension and compression rod. It is a very simple concept, a devilishly clever assembly. It is a modified bucket that does not completely contain and enfold the occupant. It is also a mobile design, a deceptively simple, three-dimensional structure capable of springing and moving with the seated person. It also allows the person to fling a leg or arm aside or to move in it.

A new chair that gives one a truly three-dimensional float is another tension chair, a 1976 Ross Miller design which promises mobile floating without instability.

Both of these designs can be easily assembled or disassembled. They give the feeling of floating without the mechanical disadvantage and bulk of the throne-floater mentioned earlier.

There are two kinds of attachment. A person can attach him/herself to a chair easily if the chair has arms. It is even possible to grasp the seats of some chairs; and some people twine their legs around chair legs.

It is much harder to attach a chair to a person. One way is to stick the person in a pocket or bucket in which there is a close fit. Another is to use straps.

Examples of attachment exist in the automobile in which the driver attaches him/herself to the steering wheel while strapped to the car and seated in a bucket.

Writers and diners may also attach themselves, in their cases to a desk or table, but using an edge rather than a bucket as a chair support.

Homo sapiens have a flexible body. Their structure is a linkage of small compression members strung with tension members (muscles and tendons). The back has sometimes been thought of as a bridge structure. Actually, it is quite different in function because our assembly of bones is flexible. Where a bridge has monumental stabile abutments from which it hangs, our bodies, in contrast, have flexible legs supporting our body structure.

With our flexible bodies, it is possible to sit in almost any chair for at least a short time, whatever the geometry of the chair. A person can adapt, then move out of it, or move *in* it.

To analyze the dynamics of people in chairs, we ask the questions: What is the structure or anatomy of the chair? What will the chair force me to do? What positions can I take on or in the chair? Is the chair safe or will I overturn and fall out? Might the chair break or be damaged? The solution is always dynamic.

"I believe that chairs should either enable a person to move about in the chair or require the person to move. Peter Cooper's wrought iron spring-bucket chair (1850) gives a person a two-dimensional motion, but Ross Miller's tension chair (1976) gives a seated person a three-dimensional, active motion, the antithesis of the fitted, posture chair—the stabile."—Blade

Photographs by Michael Pateman.

Zographos

Designing chairs is a difficult job, but describing the process is even harder. We deal with a utilitarian object that makes reference to the human body—or *should.* But I see the challenge of designing a chair in terms of *form* first, as a sitting device second. And that is because I am by now convinced that a chair is always the result of a number of compromises; they have to do with such realities as budgets, available technology, materials, and distribution, as well as other limitations. But the biggest frustration is that a chair is supposed to accommodate the human figure in the *unnatural* position of sitting, which in itself is the worst compromise.

Designing chairs is definitely not a science. Anatomy experts have advanced theories and measurements that are supposed to make the designer's life easier, but these are measurements of the average male body and the average female body and they leave out all the nonaverage. So they can serve only as mere guidelines, because there are hardly two people with identical bodies or, what is more important, two people that *sit* the same way.

The result is that there is no chair that is perfectly comfortable for everyone, but there are certainly many unnecessarily ugly chairs around and very, very few beautiful ones, whether they sit well or not. So while I try to build a certain degree of comfort into my chairs, I see greater difficulty in working out relationships in terms of materials, details, and proportions that will result in a pleasing, inviting, nonaggressive form.

The photographs of my work that follow try to show that form both in its entirety and its detail elements.

I place chairs into two general categories—the two-dimensional chair and the three-dimensional chair.

The two-dimensional chair can be wholly represented two-dimensionally. Like toothpaste extruded from its tube, it is a linear drawing of the side elevation from which the chair can be built. One knows well the result *before* the chair is made.

The three-dimensional chair is impossible to draw with any degree of accuracy until *after* the chair is built. Work-

Nicos Zographos is an internationally noted architectural, interior and furniture designer. He was born in Athens, Greece, in 1931, leaving in 1949 to be educated in the U.S. while Greece was engulfed in civil war. While studying at the State University of Iowa he took a course in Industrial Design with Professor John Shulze, whom he now credits as his major career influence. He returned frequently to Greece to work during a five-year association with the architectural firm Skidmore Owings and Merrill. Dissatisfied with quality production standards in his homeland, he started his own design and manufacturing firm, Zographos Designs Ltd., in New York in 1964.

. . . I see the challenge of designing a chair in terms of *form* first, as a sitting device second . . . a chair is always the result of a number of compromises . . . budgets, available technology, materials and distribution, as well as other limitations. But the biggest frustration is that a chair is supposed to accommodate the human figure in the *unnatural* position of sitting, which in itself is the worst compromise.

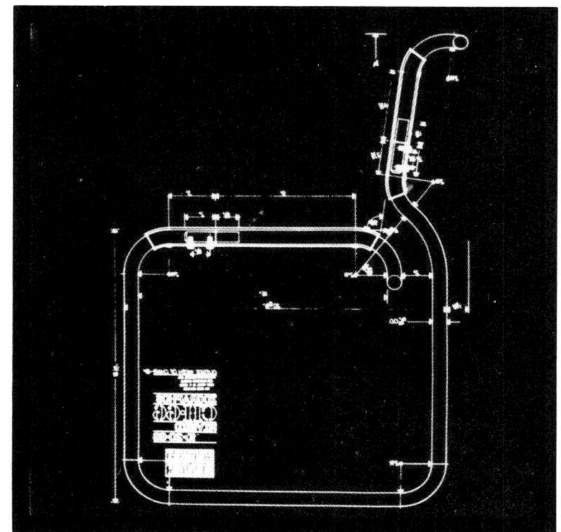

ing on chairs with a molded three-dimensional look is very much like the task of a sculptor working in the round.

Two-dimensional or three-, my criteria for a valid chair would have to satisfy standards in the following areas: form and definition; rounded, no sharp edges; economy in line and surface; compatible textures and color; articulated joints and details; a minimum number of materials; a free-standing object in space; quality and precision in manufacture; and that elusive concern for the human body.

Let us look first at the two-dimensional chairs.

This particular chair goes back to the tradition that was pioneered in the early twenties by the architects Marcel Breuer, Mies van der Rohe, and Le Corbusier. Obviously I

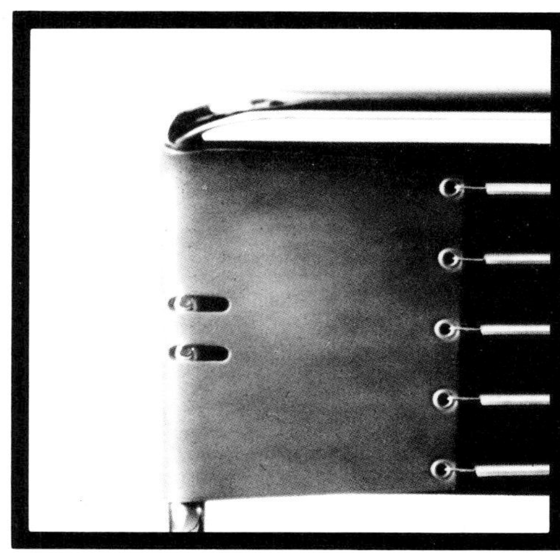

find it legitimate to borrow old principles, and let me add that almost every designer since then has done just that, some with more success than others. I believe this chair to be a development from the Bauhaus classics in its use of a double cantilever which frees both the seat and the back to move independently of each other. It is made of four pieces of tube, bent, two and two. Tooling for the bends is kept to a minimum; the assembly is mechanical, eliminating the costlier welding method, and the parts can conceivably be knocked down. The leather seat and back are held together in tension by springs, a direct debt to Corbu's early models. The exposed bolts in the back keep the frame together and the leather back from sliding down. The chair is resil-

(Above) CH.66 side chair, now in permanent collection at the Museum of Modern Art. All furniture on these pages available from Zographos Designs Limited, New York City.

. . . there is no chair that is perfectly comfortable for everyone, but there are certainly many unnecessarily ugly chairs around and very, very few beautiful ones, whether they sit well or not. So while I try to build a certain degree of comfort into my chairs, I see greater difficulty in working out relationships in terms of materials, details, and proportions that will result in a pleasing, inviting, nonaggressive form.

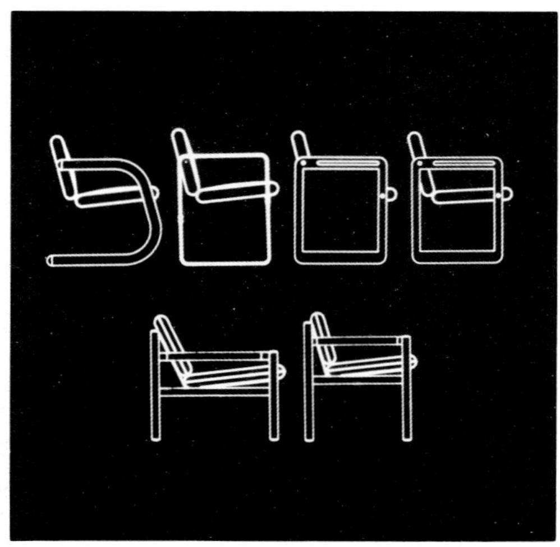

ient and elastic and because of its lightness it does not encumber space with its mass.

Many factors go into the design of production chairs, and one very important one is the use of common (identical) parts for a number of different chairs.

These chairs are a case in point in that they all use the same seat and back assembly with totally different suspension structures.

This makes for production economies in packaging, the stocking of fewer parts, and interchangeability. Two-dimensional chairs are more easily adaptable to this idea. Here we have a wood cradle; here with sides filled with panels; here a heavy tube cantilever; and here bent steel

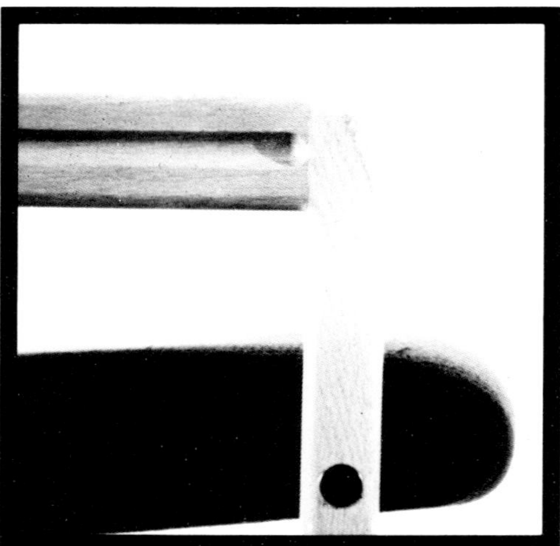

(Above) CH.15P auditorium chair, and CH.15 conference/dining armchair. (Right page) CH.17 conference/dining chair, and CH.16 conference/dining chair.

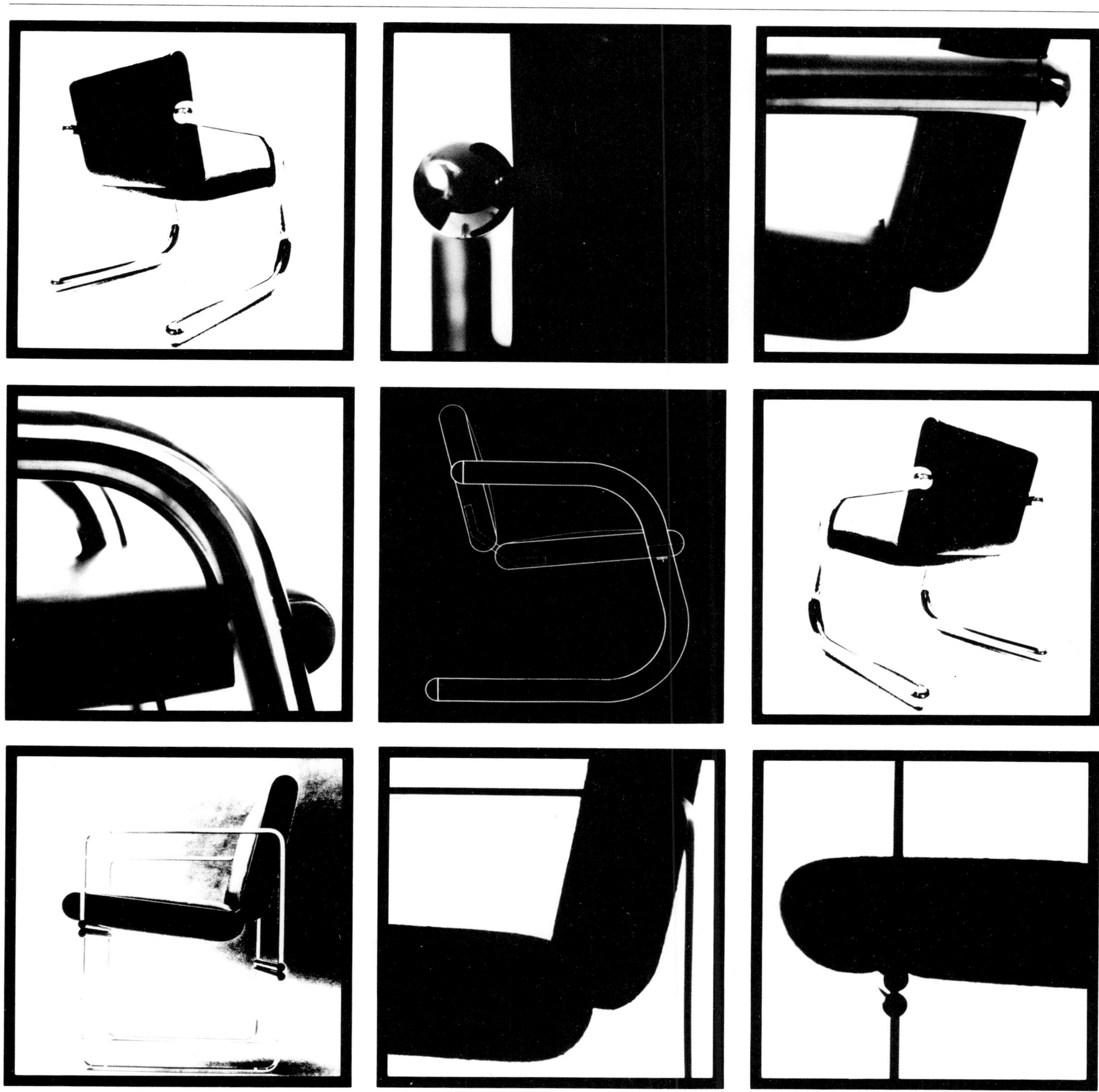

"The Modern (chairs) look so perfectly machined and proportioned that architects will usually forsake their posture and buy them anyway."—Roger Yee, "Slouching Towards Barcelona", *Progressive Architecture,* February 1975.

I place chairs into two general categories—the two-demensional chair and the three-dimensional chair. The two-dimensional chair can be wholly represented two-dimensionally. Like toothpaste extruded out of its tube, it is a linear drawing of the side elevation from which the chair can be built. One knows well the result *before* the chair is made.

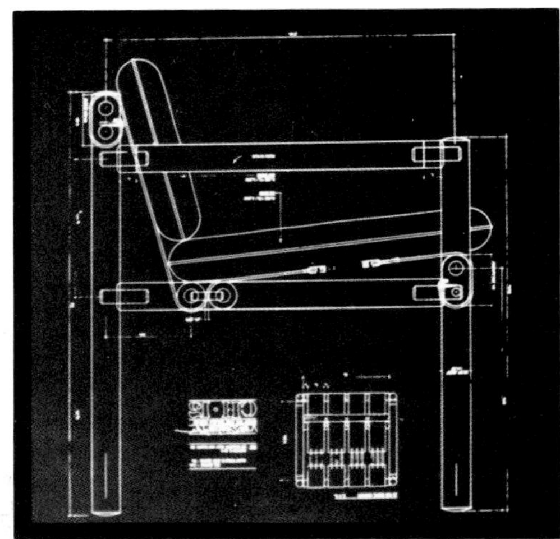

bars, four different versions of which are mechanically connected with the use of four identical tubes.

I will not claim to be particularly concerned with production costs or ease of manufacture, but still, the idea of interchangeability is intriguing and challenging.

Another suspension seat and back, only here the cushions are soft and are in turn supported by leather straps—very simple chairs made of heavy wood dowels that use leather to wrap the arms, to cover the seat and back, and to support the cushions.

We must not forget that any surface raised off the floor is the basic seat.

These three benches, one very soft, the second soft, and

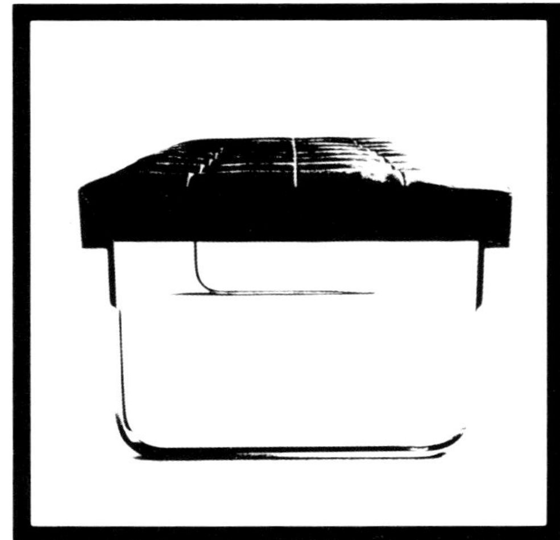

(Top) CH.12 conference/dining armchair and CH.12L lounge armchair, (above left) BE.1 bench, and (above right) BE.2 bench. (Right page top) BE.12 bench, and (below) CH.11 conference/dining armchair.

The three-dimensional chair is impossible to draw with any degree of accuracy until *after* the chair is built. Working on chairs with a molded three-dimensional look is very much like the task of a sculptor working in the round.

the third hard but with a slightly curved wood top, are the purest manifestation of seating.

And now the three-dimensional chair:

The traditional four-legged chair goes back thousands of years with few basic changes.

It is closest to sculpture. The material itself—wood—is ideal for carving into subtly formed surfaces but only where it comes in contact with the human back, and it is very much structural and architectonic where used to support the seat and back of the chair.

These are really three-dimensional objects and make it extremely difficult to arrive at a comfortable solution—relatively comfortable, that is—because the material is

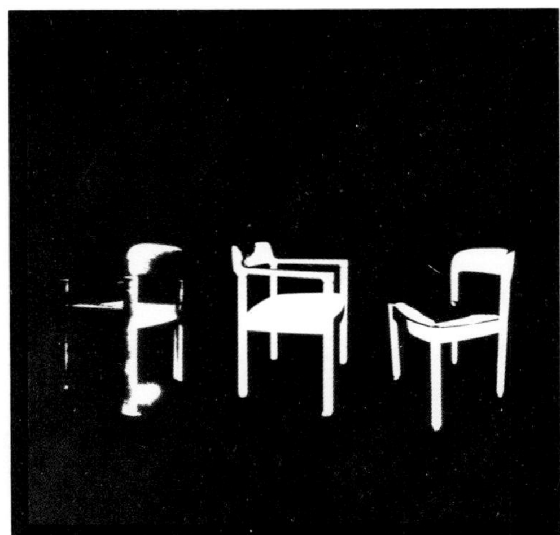

(Top) CH.11 conference/dining armchair with insert back, and (above) CH.21 dining armchair. (Right page top) CH.10 armless chair and ST.11 bar stool, and (below) CH.32TC high back bucket with tilt casters.

There are no magic formulas to get the right combination for the curve of the back and the pitch of the seat.

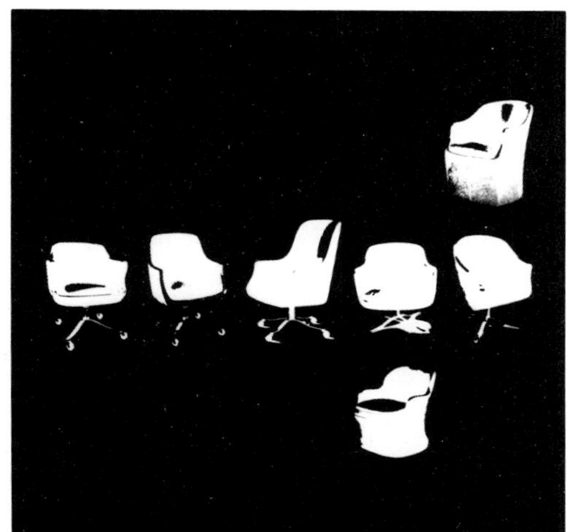

hard and has to be shaped with sensitivity and care. There are no magic formulas to get the right combination for the curve of the back and the pitch of the seat.

We get now into the series that I call "bucket chairs," all with the same metal base. Like the previous wood chairs, these have to be developed without a drawing, in the form of a model, a full-size model. I start out with a wood frame that is roughly what I have in mind, then refine it with a rasp. A number of models later, after they are upholstered and stripped and reupholstered and restripped—and with a certain amount of luck—I may end up with what I wanted. It is a lengthy process.

The base is neutral, a mutation of Mies's X-shaped glass

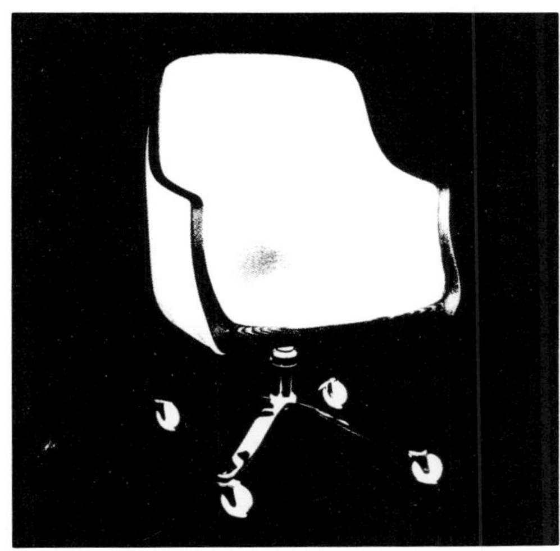

I will not claim to be particularly concerned with production costs or ease of manufacture, but still, the idea of interchangeability is intriguing and challenging.

table and X-shaped chair side supports. Structurally it is universal enough to be made in all sizes—as table bases, for example—and materials, like stainless steel, bronze, aluminum. The curves suggest tension and at the same time resiliency and repose.

With the addition of several mechanical devices like wheels, swivels, or tilts, the bucket chairs stop being static and assume rotation and oscillation, movements that keep the body from getting tired. With these chairs and their moving bases, body and chair work together.

Recently I have been working on a reinforced molded plastic base that would cover the wheels. The material is semiflexible urethane, like hard rubber. I believe that we

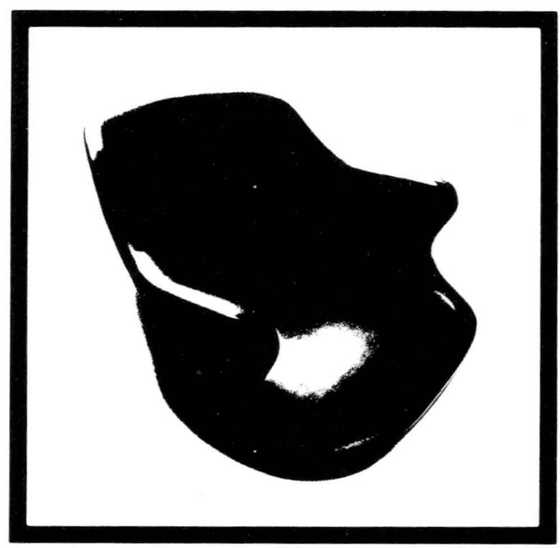

(Top) CH.2S bucket swivel chair, (middle) CH.2TC bucket chair, and (above) CH.72S English bucket swivel chair. (Right page, top) CH.4 lounge bucket chair and CH.3TC high back bucket, (middle) Ch.22 club bucket chair, and (bottom) SC.8 secretarial chair and ST.2 swivel stool.

"There were many people who visited me in my Zographos-designed office at Lois Holland Callaway and wondered out loud when it would be finished. Honest. . . . But the Zographos look was precisely what I *wanted* to achieve. Its pristine battleship ambience was sublime in conception and perfect in execution, bathed in the warmth and clarity of natural light."—George Lois, President, Creamer Lois FSR Inc.

I believe that we must totally get away from hard surfaces and sharp edges and begin to round out forms as much as possible, to make chairs from top to bottom, easier to live with and to come in contact with.

must totally get away from hard surfaces and sharp edges and begin to round out forms as much as possible, to make chairs easier to live with and to come in contact with.

The beauty of urethane foam systems is that they enable us to get structure, comfort, *and* skin—one texture, one look—out of the same material, plus that the entirely molded operation eliminates the staggering amount of handwork that still goes into the making of today's chairs.

The material happens not to be quite ready; technology is not there. But there is little doubt that a new material such as this—a new process—will result in new chair forms and will get us out of the Bauhaus-inspired period that we are still very much in today.

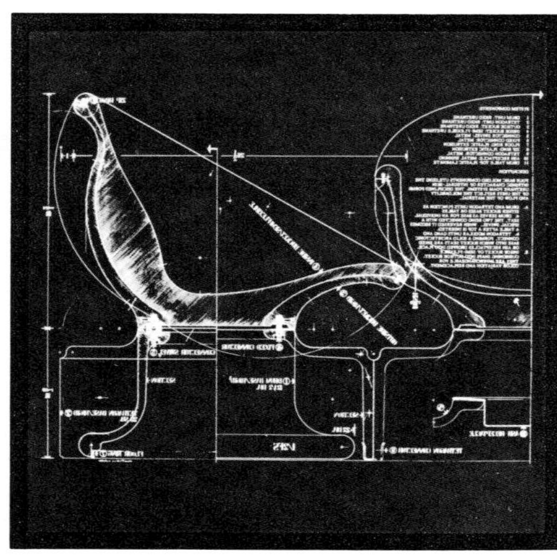

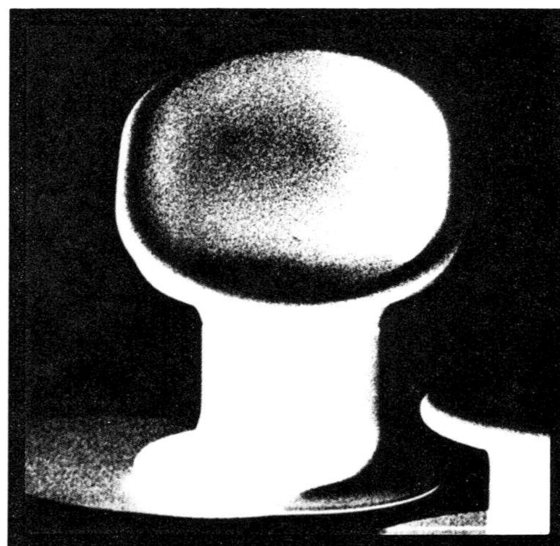

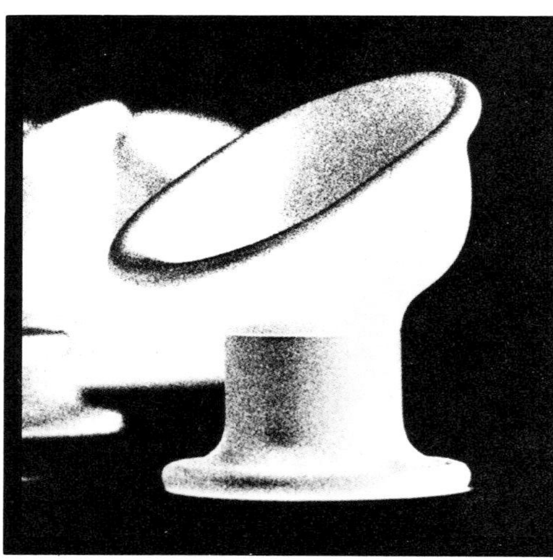

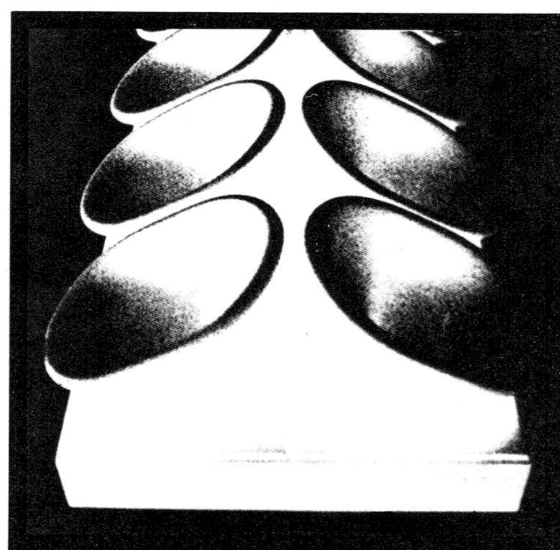

(Top) CH.72TC English bucket chair with new plastic base. (Above) new prototype made of urethane foam, with four basic molded components reflecting the flexibility of the material. Drum and tetragon units serve as bucket bases or tables when tops are inserted, inside bucket of colored semi-flexible cushioning snaps into rigid outside bucket.

(Above and right page) MS.30 lounge armchair, made of individually upholstered components. Seats, arms, backs, and cushions assemble easily to create single or multiple seating units.

All furniture photographs by Carl Fischer, except details by Nicos Zographos. Photographs of Zographos by Michael Pateman.

Gratz

I have been fabricating chairs now for 21 years. We've produced quantity and we've made prototypes—two completely different processes. I'm only the metalworker, but for the purposes of this lecture I took photographs of the wooden framework and the upholstery process, just to let you know how much actually goes into the making of one chair. The slides you will see comprise a labor period of 11 man-hours. It was staggering to me to discover how many individual hand operations are required to make a chair.

This is the chair we'll be talking about. We call it the "CH2" by Nicos Zographos. First we will deal with the base.

The raw steel comes into my shop looking like this, the ends having been rounded off in a large press with punching dies.

The first thing we do is clean the ragged ends off.

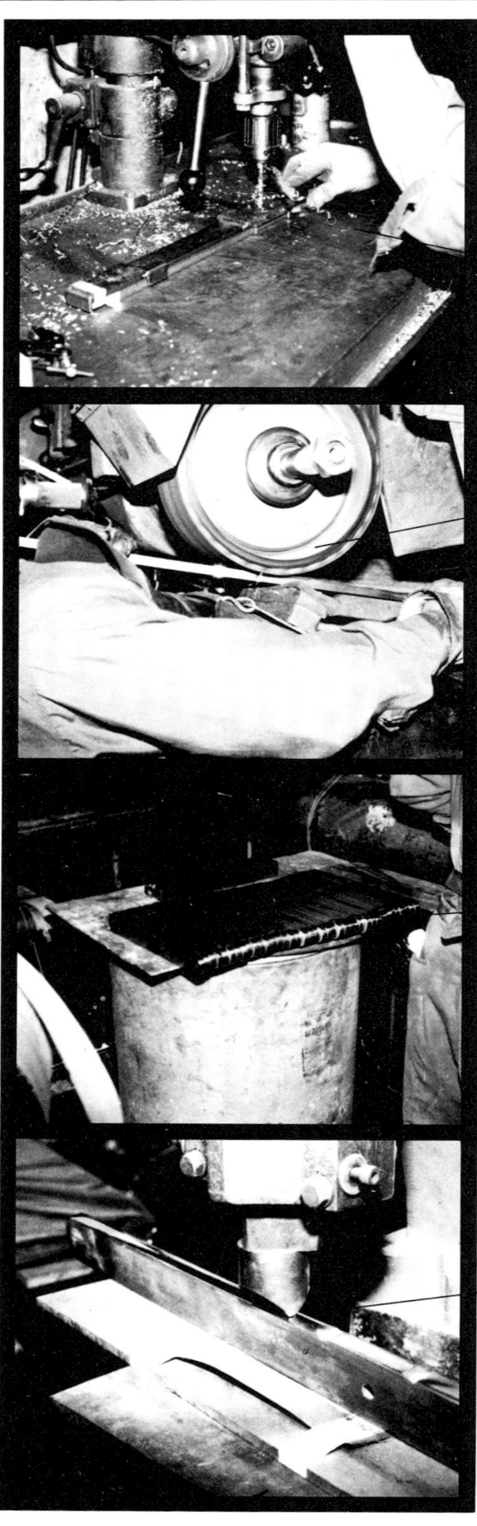

Don Gratz was born in New York City in 1934. He received a B.S. in Chemistry from St. Lawrence University, and started work in the family firm, Treitel-Gratz, founded by his father in 1929. Initially the company specialized in architectural wood and metal work, expanded into chairs through government contracts during World War II, and soon became what many designers consider the finest contract metal furniture maker in the country. They made the first Barcelona Chair in the United States in 1948 and eventually contracted to produce the entire Knoll furniture line. The company has also produced sculpture in stainless steel, brass and bronze, such as the monumental Ezio Martinelli work on the U.N. General Assembly Building, and other works by Noguchi, Sol Lewitt, and Walter de Maria.

Then we start drilling,

and, finally, polish the metal.

A stack of finished bars, semifinished really, as you will see.

And then the trade name gets stamped in.

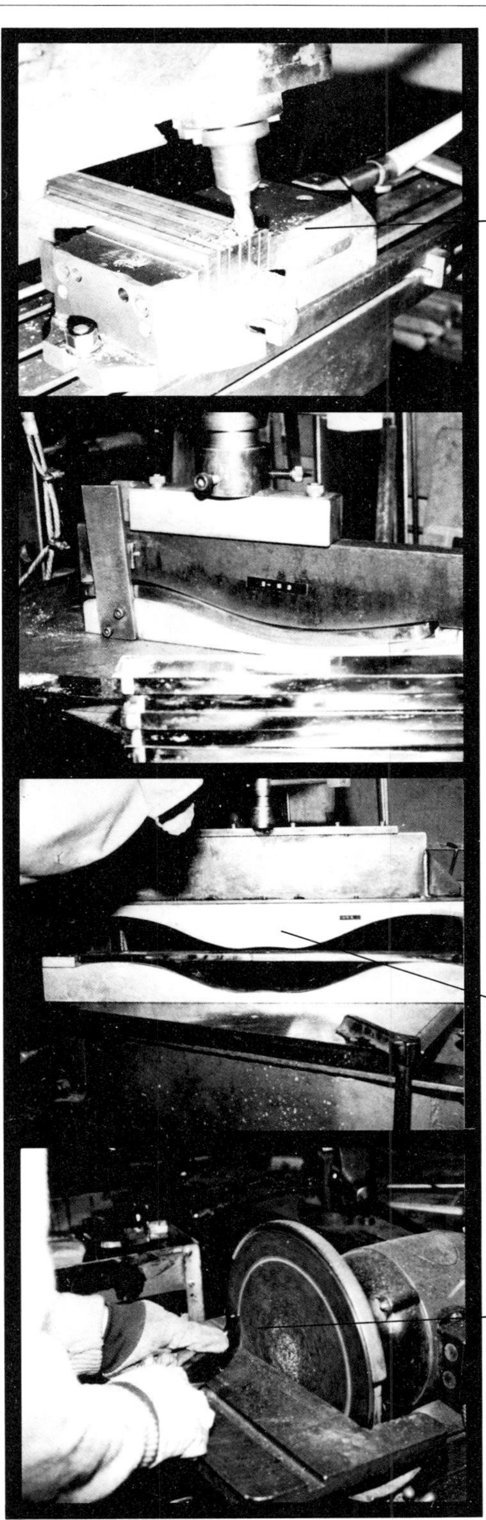

Now we prepare for the welding. First we put a groove at the edge. I'll explain the reason in a minute.

Then the chairs are bent into shape with

two different tools—one for the long bar and another for the two short bars. The shape you see now has yet nothing to do with the finished form, but with a jig we can press the chairs to the shape we want. It took two to three days to get the jig made properly for this chair. The job takes about 25 tons of pressure.

We then bevel the ends to prepare the bars for welding.

First photograph by Carl Fischer; upholstery photographs by Nicos Zographos; remainder by Donald Gratz.

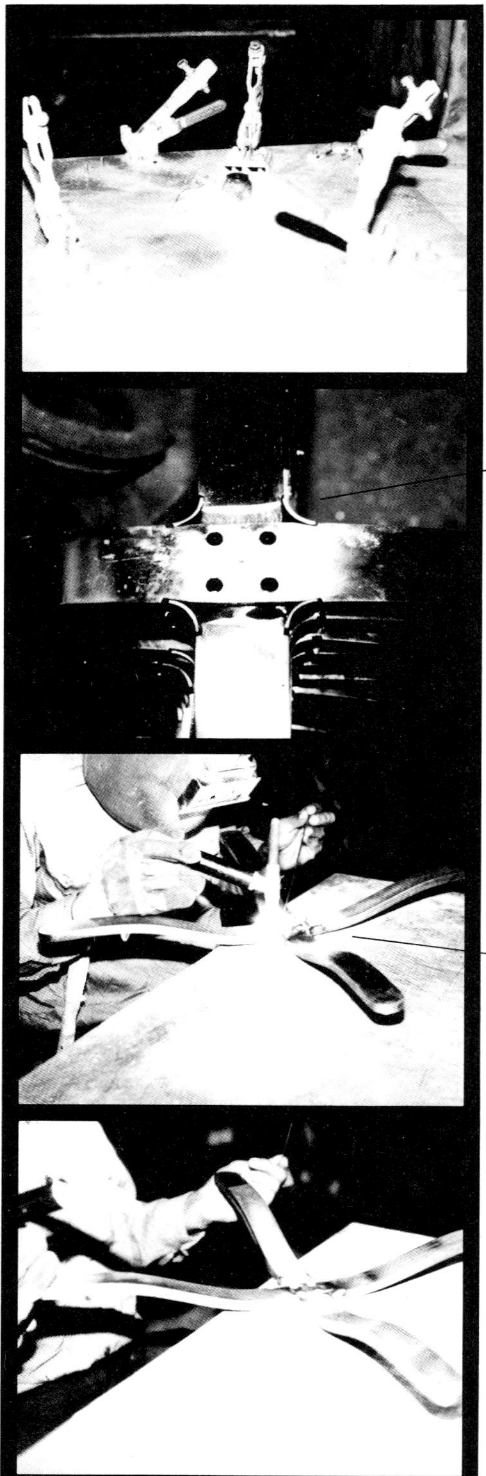

The welder puts the four pieces together in his jig,

and the little groove we pointed out earlier enables him to weld a small piece of sheet metal into each of the four corners, so that when the chair is finished all four fillets will be exactly the same.

Then he fills up the spaces,

and the welding is completed.

Approximately 20 craftsmen work in the Treitel-Gratz metal shop, 10 to 11 men usually work on any one chair.

The bottom and the top are now ground.

The top must be absolutely flat so that the column will stand vertical.

Then we start working on the corners. They're ground, filed, and sandpapered (emory-clothed, actually) until they're smooth enough to go to the polisher.

At this point we have to drill the large hole in the center for the swivel-tilt mechanism. Each one is carefully checked for proper height and angle,

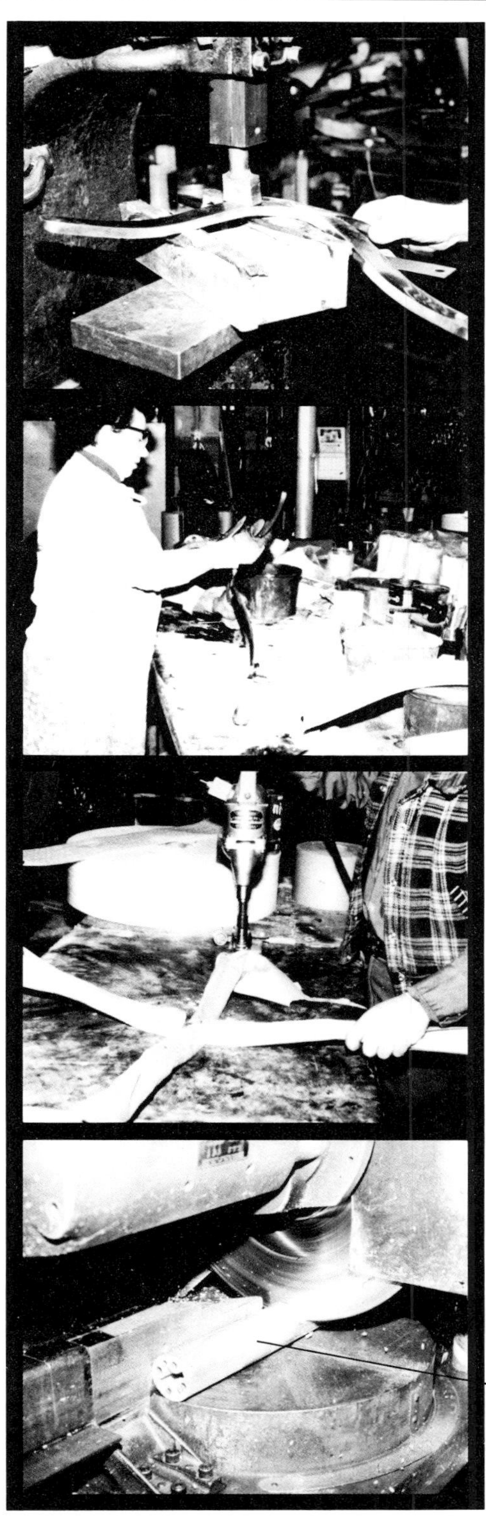

and what needs to get straightened gets straightened.

Then back for final polishing and washing and wrapping.

After they are wrapped, we put on whatever is required for casters, if indeed the chairs get casters.

Then the base is put aside while we make the column. We have been making enough of these chairs so that it is now practical to have our own aluminum extrusion for the columns. We just cut this one up.

Treitel-Gratz began using aluminum column extrusions in chair bases in 1969. They save time (ten minutes per chair), but their greatest merit is the savings in weight over traditional manufacturing methods. The use of the aluminum extrusion on a bar stool for example, reduces its weight by 25 pounds, from 50 pounds to 25.

We drive hardened steel inserts into the end to accept the screws and press the parts together. Then we press on a sleeve of bronze or stainless steel and wait for final assembly.

At last, everything goes together. The mechanism goes on, as does the proper metal sleeve, and we bolt the thing together. And that's it.

If the base is bronze, it comes in a different form. First, we get a rough casting, and it is *very* rough.

Again, it is drilled, and after all the other operations,

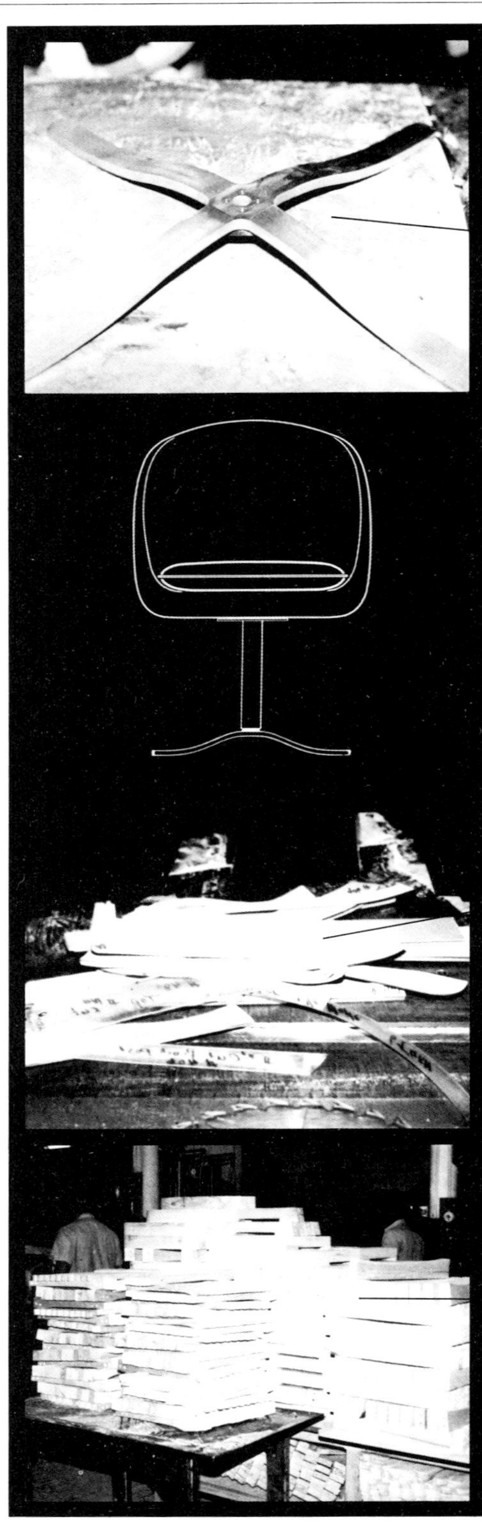

The cost of raw materials for a stainless or aluminum chair is about $20. Add another $11 to $14 for the swivel or swivel-tilt mechanism, casters (if any) and miscellaneous hardware. If bronze casting with a bronze column is required add an additional $34, plus another $5 to $6 if oxidizing is required for an antique finish.

the base eventually looks like this, or it can be polished or oxidized. That's my end of the business, but to follow the chair through all its processes, I went next to the frame maker. Nicos has always said a chair can't be drawn before it's made, so after the prototype is built,

the framemaker makes a drawing.

Then he makes templates of each piece so that they will be identical when cut.

Here are 200 chairs waiting to be put together.

They start with glue, and two men who assemble the back,

hold it together with temporary metal clamps,

and then put on the seat and the arm.

The whole thing is tightened in a vise. An airplane cargo strap is used as a clamp around the perimeter of the frame.

"I feel strongly that manufacturers do not have the right to adjust any design from the original without the designer's consent. Even with advanced technology, most changes are simply to save money and remain unjustified."—Gratz

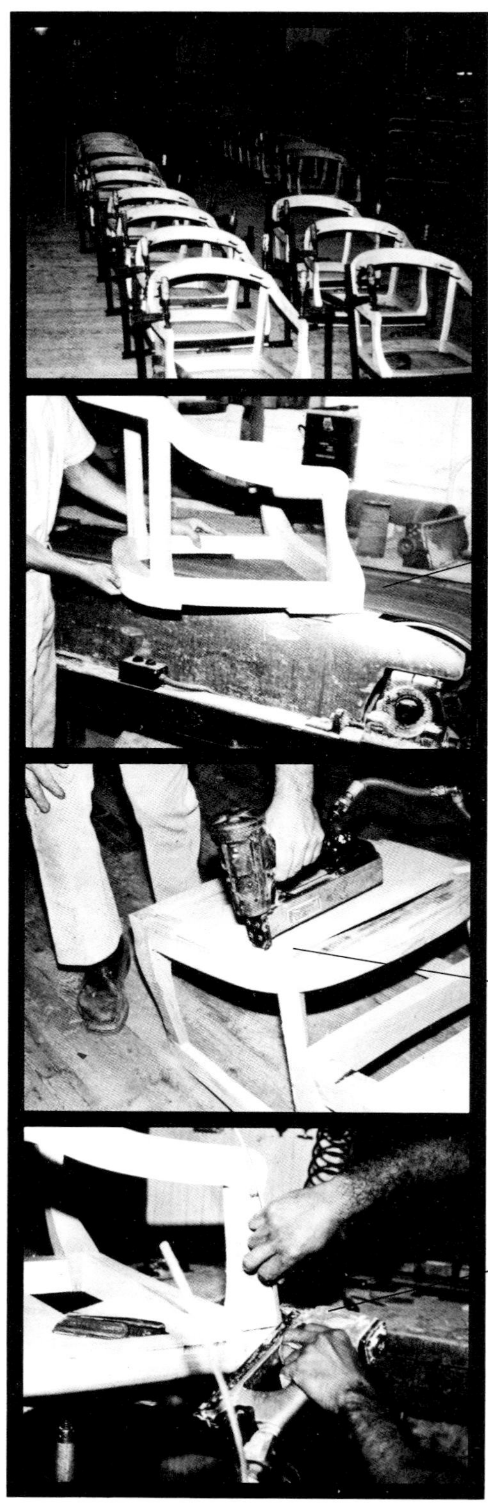

And these are frames waiting for the glue to set before the next operations—

sandpapering, to clean off the parts that don't exactly meet;

attaching the bottom temporarily;

and putting on the edge used by the upholsterer as a fabric stop. Then the chair is covered in foam by the upholsterer.

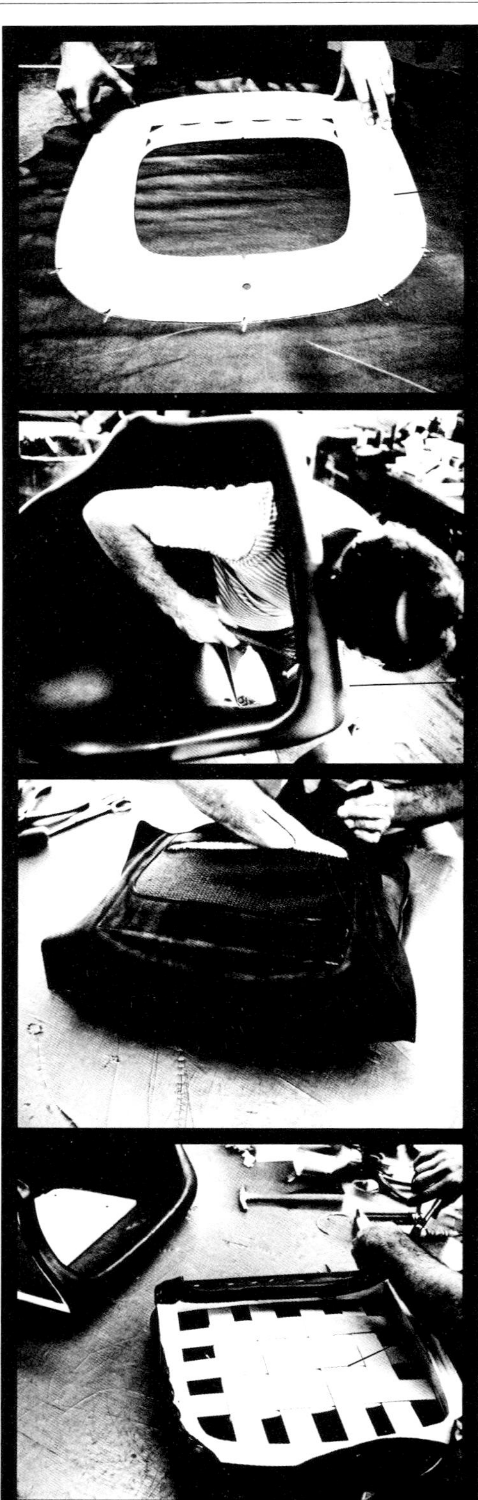

Meanwhile, the cutter marks and cuts all the pattern pieces from templates he has worked out over the course of time. Then he sews them, five thicknesses plus the newspaper to help the fabric slide over the sewing table. The cushion is trimmed,

and then the upholsterer really goes to work on the chair. The whole covering of this chair is constructed of one piece of leather after sewing, so from the inside there is considerable stretching and pulling, not only of the leather but of the upholsterer.

He stuffs and sews the cushion,

inserts it, then screws back the piece that the framemaker had originally put on. The cushion goes into the chair with staples to clip it in place.

The upholsterer now moves to the outside, where he attaches the blind nailing strip, carefully taping it so it won't cut the leather,then squeezing the foam and leather in with a little tool. He then closes the seam very carefully by hand. He finishes stapling the bottom, screws the base on, and the chair is ready for some satisfied customer.

I've put up these last two slides just to show you that we do make other chairs for fun. I made a Barcelona chair, a unique one, very small . . .

and a full-size one. . . .

Anywhere between 25 to 100 chairs are done in one production run, depending upon orders and availability of materials. One hundred chair bases would take one thousand man hours, or approximately two months, to produce. All work is done in the Treitel-Gratz factory in Queens, New York. Completed units are sent to outside contractors for upholstery.

Stendig

Charles Stendig is currently an independent design and marketing consultant and no longer holds any interest in the company he founded, Stendig, Inc. He was born in 1924 in New York City, received an M.A. degree in International Trade from the University of Mexico, and began his importing career as a "tail end" tradesman specializing in fish liver oils. He eventually became a furniture road salesman, then a manufacturer's representative for several California furniture makers. His own importing business began after his timely meeting, in a bar, of a Finnish government representative—the results being the first Finnish furniture imported to America. His unique business adventures have taken him to many countries, notably Switzerland for the classic Bauhaus originals, and to Italy for the fun and surreal.

. . .designers, and dealers are constantly looking for chairs for specific purposes, chairs that fit into the spirit of the particular decor they envision. It was the purpose of our company and companies like ours to supply these chairs.

My former company was primarily a specialized manufacturer and importer of seating. In fact, seating and tables made up practically the entire collection, very different from what we call a full-time furniture company. It was further specialized in that it serviced a relatively small market. The commercial furniture market is a very large one. The company dealt primarily with interior designers, architects, industrial designers, space planners, and dealers—all professionals involved in furnishing residential and commercial interior spaces.

About 20 percent of our furniture was used for residential installations and approximately 80 percent was used for commercial installations—that is, libraries, colleges, hotels, offices, every place except the home. Architects, interior designers, and dealers are constantly looking for chairs for specific purposes, chairs that fit into the spirit of the particular decor they envision. It was the purpose of our company and companies like ours to supply these chairs.

The American furniture manufacturers and American importers that supply chairs to this particular market fall into two general categories: companies offering a homogeneous collection—that is, a family grouping of furniture representing a single design philosophy of furniture, that can easily be grouped in a single interior—and those companies offering a heterogeneous collection, models differing widely both in their design philosophy and in the materials used for their construction.

Our company fell into the second category, in that it presented chairs made of a very wide range of materials. We utilized plate glass, plastics, steel, aluminum, molded foam (both hard and soft), solid and laminated wood, as well as bentwood in the production of our chairs.

Our chairs represented varying design viewpoints and philosophies; they represented the work of some fifty designers from a half-dozen European countries and the United States.

I believe that there are many roads to good de-

(Left page) Stendig's Pony, designed by Eero Aarnis. Reinforced molded urethane foam and upholstered. An entire herd of ponies exists today around the boardroom table of a certain (and shy) large midwestern corporation, as part of the architect's original specifications. (Above) The Sassi Rocks, seats also made of molded polyurethane foam.

While touring in Italy, Stendig heard of a group of architects led by Giuseppi Raimondi. They worked in a tiny factory in the foothills of the Alps, experimenting with modern, eccentric furniture forms like the Pony and Cactus. Fascinated, Stendig was receptive to sculptural forms by the Finn Eero Aarnis and he marketed them simply because he liked them.

The furniture market in the United States is divided into two categories—residential and contract. The annual wholesale contract market is presently about 4 billion dollars. The residential market approaches 6.5 billion.

(Above) "Joe", two seat sofa on casters designed by DePas, D'Urbino and Lomazzi. Foam upholstered in natural leather. (Top right) "Marilyn", love seat designed by Studio 65. Molded urethane foam covered in lipstick red stretch nylon fabric. All furniture (except Rocks) available at Stendig Inc., New York City.

. . . we liked to think of our company as a fine hardware or jewelry store supplying a collection of carefully preselected chairs that . . . represented the finest design available in the world. We're were extremely proud of the chairs in our collection. It took us twenty years to gather them together. They represented a lifetime of work.

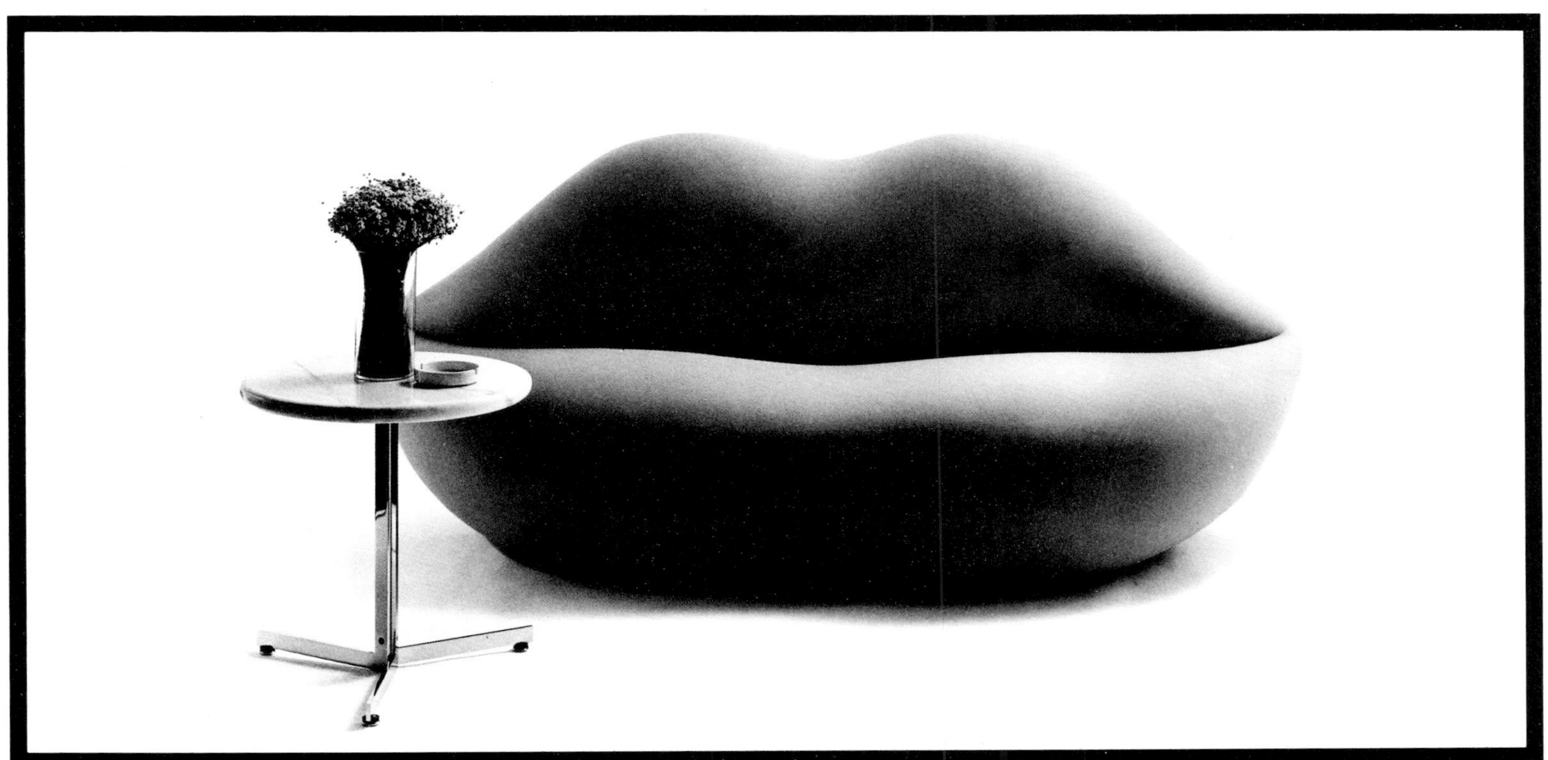

sign and we liked to think of our company as a fine hardware or jewelry store supplying a collection of carefully preselected chairs that, in our eyes, represented the finest design available in the world. We were extremely proud of the chairs in our collection. It took us 20 years to gather them. They represented a lifetime of work.

Some of these models were extremely popular, sold very well—thousands of pieces each year—and have been extensively copied by other manufacturers. Other models, equally valid in our eyes, sold only a dozen or so pieces a year. We continued to carry such models because our company played an important bellwether role in the marketplace. It was expected of us to bring forth the new, the experimental, and the avant-garde. On the other hand we were not a publicly endowed foundation but a commercial company and had to produce a profit in return for our labors. Bear in mind that primarily we imported products made for us. We had only limited manufacturing facilities of our own. Where then did the design, the product, come from? We had exclusive American distribution and sales contracts with a number of European furniture factories. These factories were leaders in contemporary furniture design and they commissioned important design talent. We imported from companies such as DeSede in Switzerland, Asko in Finland, Thonet in Czechoslovakia, and Gufram in Italy.

Working with these factories was primarily a two-way street. We selected designs from their collections, often altering them somewhat to suit the American market. For example, in the German market, office chairs are required by law to have a five-pronged or five-legged base. These are not very popular in America, so our own staff of designers usually redesigned the bases or any other parts to make them more suitable, more adaptable, more salable in the American market.

We were also in the business of bringing together designers and manufacturers. We found

The first-run guarantee (200 to 500 pieces, at a minimum investment of $10,000) was particularly attractive to factories in Italy, Switzerland, Finland, Sweden and Hong Kong—places not yet known for furniture production, and unaccustomed to the evaluation of new designs. Eventually, 16 to 20 factories around the world manufactured chairs for the Stendig Company.

. . . we played the role of bringing designs or designers to the factory's attention. By guaranteeing to take the first cutting or the first production run, we minimized the risk that the factory undertakes in producing this new design or in working with this new designer.

There isn't any important chair in the marketplace today that is the result of the first experiment of a designer. The long and arduous process involves many, many models to be made, changed, discarded, before the prototype is considered ready for the marketplace.

from experience that factories are often managed by production people who have a strong and intricate knowledge of furniture production but a rather less-sound knowledge of design. So we played the role of bringing designs or designers to the factory's attention. By guaranteeing to take the first cutting or the first production run, we minimized the risk that the factory undertakes in working with this new design or this new designer.

What we generally received in return for our labors was the right of first refusal on any new designs that resulted from such a collaboration.

In addition, our firm maintained direct contact with free-lance designers in many countries, reviewing their latest designs for possible inclusion in our collection. Some of the free-lance designers we worked with were Ilmari Tapiovaara and Eero Aarnio in Finland; Carl Erik Ekselius and his son, Jan Ekselius, in Sweden; Robert Haussmann, Bruno Rey, and Edlef Bandixen in Switzerland; Eleonora Peduzzi Riva, Giuseppe Raimondi, and Tito Agnoli in Italy. And in America we worked with Elena and Massimo Vignelli and with Wendell Castle.

Since it usually takes a minimum of one year (and very often two, three, or four) to produce a good chair, we kept in constant touch as a product developed in each designer's workshop. There isn't any important chair in the marketplace today that is the result of the first experiment of a designer. The long and arduous process requires many, many models to be made, changed, discarded, before the prototype is considered ready for the marketplace. Even after a chair reaches the market, it constantly undergoes change in the form of small mechanical or structural changes based on feedback after the chair goes into use. The original Barcelona chair in the Tugendhat House at Brno, Czechoslovakia, has from a distance the same configuration and appearance as the model currently in production. But when you examine the details carefully, you'll note important changes made

". . . when the Italians kicked the Bauhaus in the seat of its ideological pants, they did so with humor. Sometimes the cushions became the whole chair . . . others, lovingly handmade, looked less like furniture than like species from a cosmic bestiary."—Roger Yee, "Slouching Towards Barcelona", *Progressive Architecture,* February 1975.

The Tugendhat House, located outside Brno, Czechoslovakia, was designed by the architect Mies van der Rohe in 1930 as a private home. It was furnished originally with Mies-designed furniture, including the Tugendhat chair, and possibly the Barcelona chair.

A chair is a piece of sculpture. To make a new chair, a different chair, and a better chair is an extremely difficult task and it gets tougher and tougher. . . . It would seem that every form and every technique possible has been used. . . .

during the 50 years that the chair has been in production. These constant changes are made primarily to strengthen the chair and make it more adaptable.

A few years ago I visited the Tugendhat House in Brno, Czechoslovakia, now a children's hospital. The interior is still very well maintained; unfortunately, the original furniture has been preempted by local architects since the socialist state took it over. If you search the world hard enough you can still find the original designs. There is quite a visual difference between the old models and the new ones. This process goes on constantly. I don't think that there's any designer, even after his model goes into production (Nicos can correct me if he feels he's the exception), who doesn't make regular, small changes, improvements basically in the structure of the piece itself. And as new techniques develop, these are utilized by designers or by the factory itself with the designer's approval.

Professors of design are another source of chair ideas. Willy Guhl, who's been training Swiss furniture designers for about thirty years at the Zurich Kunstgewerbeschule, proved an excellent source of new design. I can do nothing stronger than to re-emphasize what Nicos has said: A chair is a piece of sculpture. To make a new chair, a different chair, and a better chair is an extremely difficult task and it gets tougher and tougher as time goes on. It would seem that every form and every technique possible has been used, so it becomes more and more of a difficult task.

I was delighted to hear that Nicos is entering a chair in the San Diego A.I.A. competition. We were called to submit some furniture for that competition. My first reaction was, by God, we don't need any more chairs and we are not going to submit anything! But I feel delighted that there is still work actually going on and that Nicos feels there is still lots of work to be done.

Of course, the selection of models themselves is not a science. There is generally one person in

(Top left) Elda, swivel lounge chair designed by Joe C. Colombo. Fiberglass frame upholstered in soft natural leather. (Above) Jan, chaise lounge designed by Jan Ekselius. Welded steel tube frame, flat steel inner spring suspension, covered with molded foam and zippered covers.

Willy Guhl, now in his 60's, has trained many well-known Swiss furniture designers at the Kunstgewerbeschule, as well as being a furniture designer in his own right. The school is for general design and is equivalent to Pratt Institute in New York. The AIA chair competition award-winning team of Berger-Baumeister (see page 136) was trained at the school.

There is generally one person in every company—that happened to be me—who selects the furniture on which the success or failure of the company depends. We searched the world over. We read every foreign publication we could find, looked at every design submitted to us, in trying to find a new and exciting product.

every company—that happened to be me—who selects the furniture on which the success or failure of the company depends. We search the world over. We read every foreign publication we can find, look at every design submitted to us, in trying to find a new and exciting product. I can assure you it is a long, hard, and difficult search. If we can add two or three new chairs a year to the collection, that is a lot. And those two or three pieces are screened out of literally thousands. It's a hard task. We're dealing with a critical audience, and there isn't a more critical audience than our own fellow designers. While we sometimes have questions about their judgment, we realize that they are professionals who usually know what they are doing.

The company was started in 1955 with my own survey of the market. I thought that I'd like to bring back some of the old classic chairs of the bentwood, Bauhaus, deStijl, constructivist, and secessionist eras because I felt there was a market for them. I thought that rather than try to go the expensive route of developing new designs, I would try to find some of the old classics and bring them back.

The first model I found was the old British officer's chair. I will pass the photo around. It is about the oldest "contemporary" chair we know of. We have been able to date it back to about 1840, just about the time that Michael Thonet started his bentwood business.

We have seen photographs of Teddy Roosevelt sitting in this chair on his hunting expeditions to Africa in the early part of this century. We know that British officers used it in India. Primarily it is a chair that disassembles easily; it is made without glue, held together only by leather straps. The legs, you will notice, are like tent pins, so we suspect that these chairs were originally produced out of tent pegs.

The British officer's chairs are very comfortable because you have a canvas or leather back to give you full support and to match your par-

"The designers always retained control over design changes, as written into their contracts. Nobody makes changes just to make changes; there's great cost involved. Bastardization occurs only with the copyists."—Stendig

(Above) Environ One, modular back and seat units, manufactured under license from Nikol Internazionale, Italy. Solid urethane foam of varying density, with zippered covers. (Top right) Terrazza, lounge seating designed by Ubald Klug. Dacron and structured foam, covered with leather or suede. All photographs provided by Stendig International Inc.

ticular shape. It is also a rather flexible chair that will balance itself on uneven ground; it has a swinging back which helps relieve the back muscles and gives it additional comfort. All in all, it is an exciting chair that can be rolled up and carried in a bundle.

We reintroduced this chair and had very limited success with it. We sold it for about five years and then I gave it up. The cost of the raw materials, as Nicos mentioned, reached the point where we felt it became too expensive.

Next I tried to get some of the old bentwood chairs. At that time there were no bentwood chairs coming into America. Thonet had stopped exporting them to America many years previously. There are no facilities in the United States for making really fine bentwood chairs, nor for the necessary hand caning. So I went to Czechoslovakia and convinced the Thonet people there to dust off some of their old metal molds and make some of the chairs that they had originally made many years ago.

The first chair we got into production was this, we call it the "Corbusier"-bentwood armchair. It actually wasn't designed by Le Corbusier. He was born many years after 1870, the approximate date this chair was first made. We don't know who the designer is. Some say it was Michael Thonet himself, but we're not sure. The reason that they named it "Corbusier" is that it was a chair he used in 1925 at a famous interior decorating exhibition in Paris, L'Esprit d'Art Nouveau. The chair has been associated with his name ever since. It appears in photos of his studio. The books tell us that Le Corbusier was a great chair designer, but I really have to contradict that; he never designed a chair and wasn't even terribly interested in furniture. The furniture that appears under his name was furniture designed by Charlotte Perriand in Paris and by Pierre Jeanneret, his cousin.

By the way, Charlotte Perriand is in her nineties and still lives in Paris, the last I heard. She usually is glad to show any visitor the origi-

"Thonet's merit was to have designed and manufactured a mass product of undoubted aesthetic worth, a truly social product. While William Morris was expostulating about art for all the people but producing expensive pieces for wealthy patrons, the Thonet firm achieved . . . an inexpensive, handsome product, truly available to the many."—Herwin Schaefer, *Nineteenth Century Modern,* Praeger, 1970.

The company started in 1955 with my own survey of the market. I thought that I'd like to bring back some of the old classic chairs of the bentwood, Bauhaus, deStijl, constructivist and secessionist eras because I felt there was a market for them.

nal chair drawings that bear her name. She has kept those wonderful original drawings.

I managed to find a metal mold that bore Corbusier's signature at the 112-year-old Thonet factory, which is still in operation. This is one of them. He actually went to the factory and inscribed his signature on a metal mold that he thought had the best bentwood shape. From that mold was made the chair he used at the 1925 exhibition. Since then we've reactivated a bentwood chair from Josef Hoffman, an architect. If you recall, Josef Hoffman was one of the founders of the secessionist movement in Austria at the turn of the century. He designed this chair that we call the "Prague" bentwood armchair about 1925 and it's still in production today, still made from the original molds.

We then rejuvenated one of the old bentwood rockers, not the best one, I'm afraid, but an old one nonetheless. And I'll pass these photographs around.

We had a great deal of success with the bentwood chairs—so much so that even the American Thonet went back into the importing business. Most of the bentwood chairs that you see today remain imported, mostly from Eastern European countries because of the hand labor required. It takes about 54 hours to make a single chair. That's an awful lot of time. So the next time you see these relatively inexpensive chairs, *do know* that it's the greatest bargain on the market today whether they're Stendig's chairs or someone else's chairs but only as long as the caning is done by *hand*.

Question: Did you have design training?
Stendig: No, I only have a foreign trade background. I came into this field through the back door and was one of the lucky, I guess, 5 percent of the people in this country who found the kind of work that they really love to do. I love working with designers, but I am not a designer myself, nor have I designed any of the models in our collection.

"The tradition in Europe at the beginning of the century was to give furniture design credit to the office rather than to the actual designers working within that office. Le Corbusier, not terribly interested in furniture, allowed individuals in his office to sign their own molds. Charlotte Perriand's signature remains on the original molds she designed as do those by Pierre Jeanneret, Corbusier's brother. In keeping with the tradition, individual designers in Mies' and Breuer's office were not given credit for their designs. Some sought credit for Breuer's 1926 dining chairs—Mart Stam, a Bauhaus teacher, won his claim in a West German court."—Stendig

(Top left) Corbusier bentwood armchair, designer unknown. Steam bent beech frame, hand caned. At the right in the same photograph, the Prague bentwood side chair and armchair designed by Josef Hoffman. Also steam bent beech frames, hand natural or nylon caned. Available at Stendig Inc., New York City.

The original bentwood process involves steaming long wood pieces until they are pliable enough to be bent to shape in a metal mold. They are then clamped in place and dried for at least 24 hours.

Exchange

Moderator: There's one point I want to bring out, one that everybody seemed to touch upon—the necessity of more chairs. Why do we need more chairs, especially since you all question whether there can ever be a good chair? Why do we see thousands of new chairs every year?
Zographos: Well, we need chairs to sit on, obviously, but we certainly don't need most of the chairs that are being manufactured and sold in this country; they are an insult to our intelligence. It's the same situation as in Detroit, where cars that should not be produced and sold are being produced and sold. We need a means of transportation but not the cars that we are buying. And we need chairs, but not the chairs that most merchants are selling in great quantities.
Moderator: Are you saying that there is a need for well-designed chairs?
Zographos: We need sensible, sensitive, simple chairs, not pseudo-something-else chairs. I'm talking about the mass-produced, mass-distributed market item.
Moderator: Isn't expense the reason why we don't have more well-designed chairs?
Zographos: Well, not necessarily. There are a lot of good chairs, simple, very cheap chairs. Some of the early Breuer chairs are still being manufactured and imported. Their price is reasonable.
Moderator: Do you feel that you are answering a need for a change that is prompted by fashion changes?
Stendig: I hate to think that. I believe we've got enough designs now to work with for the next ten years. There are lots of great designs in almost every area. I don't think we need more good designs. I agree with Nikos that some of the really good designs that exist should go into large-scale production so that they may become accessible to a larger number of people.

Moderator: Tell us about your baseball glove.
Stendig: Well, three Italian designers had an idea: they thought it would be fun to have a leather chair that looks like a great baseball fielder's glove. The amazing thing about it is that it is

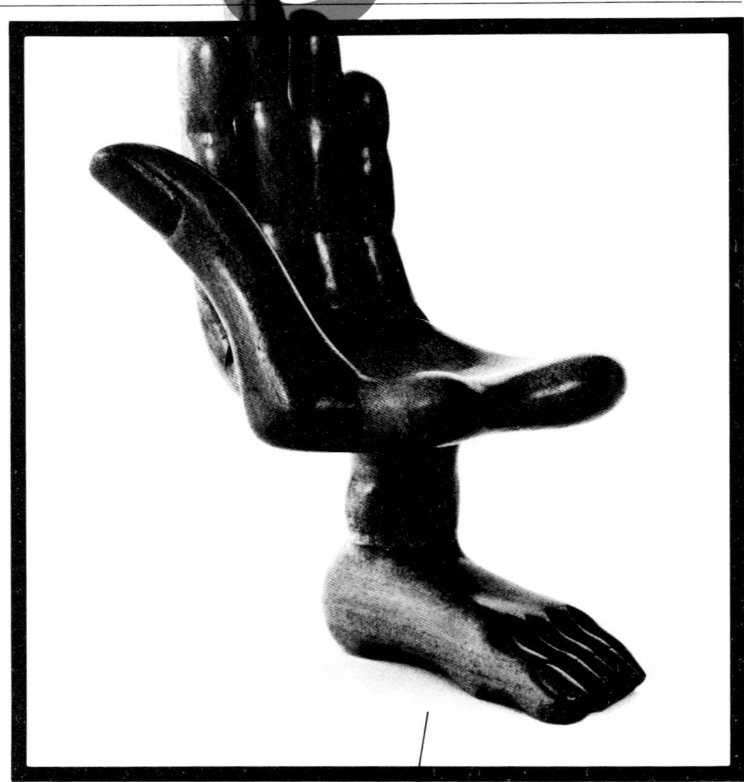

extremely comfortable. I have two of them at home, although I do not particularly like to see my own furniture in my home. They serve a limited fun use; that is what they were designed for. They are fun chairs, something we do not see very much of. There is practically no humor in furniture.

Read Clement Meademore's marvelous book. I can recommend it highly. It includes all the old great designs and some new ones and a whole section devoted to humorous furniture. And I think there's a place for it. I think the baseball glove is similar to a hand by Pedro Friedberg from Mexico. Pedro is a well-known surrealist sculptor. He shows in New York. I don't know whether you remember the foam rubber rocks we brought out. They were great to sit on, nice and firm and comfortable, and they looked exactly like boulders. You could really sit on them; you didn't sink down to the floor.

We had this gondola, which is a plastic rocker. It wasn't successful because of the difficulty in

Nicos Zographos, Don Gratz, and Charles Stendig gave their talks on the same evening. Immediately following was this panel discussion. The moderator was Peter Bradford, producer of *Chair,* and "Question" indicates queries from the audience.

Clement Meadmore's book is *The Modern Chair: Classics in Production,* Van Nostrand Reinhold Company, New York, 1975.

. . . we need chairs to sit on, obviously, but we certainly don't need most of the chairs that are being manufactured and sold in this country; they are an insult to our intelligence.—Zographos

getting in and out of it—and also the rather high price. Then we had the wedge chair, which is basically a block of solid foam rubber, just a form, with an elastic cover. It was unique in that it didn't look like a seat. You actually sat *into* the curved edge.

We brought all these pieces out to give a little humor, a little color, to the average commercial interior. The Pratone, the big grass, was great to sit on. I think we sold two in a period of two years. So maybe we should have become a foundation.

I guess our most successful fun piece was Marilyn, a love seat still in the collection. Of course Marilyn was adapted from Salvador Dali's 1935 sculpture. It is an all-molded foam piece, relatively comfortable to sit on, covered with red stretch fabric.

Moderator: Like Nicos in design, you seem to be talking about things that are not necessarily related to the utility of chairs but rather to the spirit of a piece of furniture in a space; that a sense of spirit comes before or, perhaps, is just as important to, the shape of the chair. I am talking about beautiful design, beautiful shape and form, and things like humor. Are these areas of proper emphasis for something that people usually think of as strictly a utility? Nicos?

Zographos: If you go back in the recent history of chairs, you will note that many chairs have been influenced directly by the painting and sculpture of the time. This is not the first time that we are seeing a utilitarian object like a chair take on another form, in this case pop art. A few years after pop art we see chairs that look like pop art. The same thing happened when after the deStijl movement came the Gerrit Rietveld chairs. There are others; it has been happening all along.

Moderator: Bauhaus included.

Zographos: Bauhaus included, of course, with the constructivist chairs. The emphasis was on very lightweight metal. Early Bauhaus furniture was a reflection of the prominent changes in architecture which influenced the art of the time.

". . . practically everyone who considers himself a designer or architect, including carpenters, craftsmen and producers in general, has sooner or later designed some chairs. Even if he never saw it made, you can bet he still has the design in his drawer. . . ."—Ettore Sottsass, Jr., "The Chair", *MANtransFORMS*, Cooper-Hewitt Museum, 1976.

(Left page) Pedro Friedeberg's "Handchair", photograph courtesy of the artist, Mexico City, Mexico. (Above right) "Mae West" lips sofa by Salvador Dali, photograph courtesy of the Edward James Foundation, West Sussex, England, (below left) Cevetti, Derossi, and Rosso's "Pratone" (big meadow), photograph courtesy of Stendig International Inc., New York.

When we told a designer that this chair was made of reinforced nylon, he got that glazed look in his eye, because reinforced nylon didn't mean anything to him. He didn't know the difference between reinforced nylon or polypropylene.—Stendig

Moderator: What is influencing chairs now? What movement in your eyes?

Zographos: That's a tough one. It's very difficult. I don't know the answer, but I do know that nothing much is happening in the chair design world——

Moderator: But there is!

Zographos: ——there's not much direction.

Audience question: ——the new materials that you were going to mention?

Zographos: The trouble is they're not functioning yet. When they do, the new materials will be used to bring us out of the Bauhaus era and into a new one.

Moderator: Well, if we have a new form that is semi-rigid and can be used both hard and soft for the same form, what kinds of problems does this create for Don Gratz, for example, in the production of prototypes or new chairs?

Zographos: He will have to go into new plastics.

Gratz: Right. I'll have to go into plastics. I would get out of the metal business.

Moderator: And would you?

Gratz: We have gone through plastics already. We can't go any further with plastics. I watch the world market and I know what a tough problem Nicos has. Several manufacturers in Europe have tackled the same problems using today's plastics and they also came to the conclusion that the material is not ready yet.

Moderator: But it *will* be.

Zographos: Okay, but not yet.

Gratz: The problem with a lot of designers is that to them plastics are plastics. They do not distinguish and they do not differentiate.

Stendig: Which made a problem for us. We had hard and soft plastic furniture in our collection. When we told a designer that this chair was made of reinforced nylon, he got that glazed look in his eye, because reinforced nylon didn't mean anything to him. He didn't know the difference between reinforced nylon or polypropylene. I think at the moment we have sort of *had* it with plastic furniture, including the plastic chairs you are sitting on.

Zographos: Yes. But, Charlie, what I am talking about with this plastic is exciting, not because it is plastic but——

Gratz: No, no, I know! It's what you can do with it!

Zographos: ——because it has an integral skin which can in the molding operation contain not only one but many degrees of softness or density within the same form. It's an exciting *idea.*

Gratz: I must say that these integral skins all feel like elephant hides.

Zographos: Okay, I agree with you. Granted. But——

Gratz: Who wants to sit on an elephant?

Zographos: But wait a minute. The material is going to improve with technology. We are already using it for automobile seats. And if it's used correctly, as in the VW dashboard, it's better than vinyl cover material.

Question: Do chair designers tend to specialize, really exclusively, or do you find designers of chairs who are also fairly diversely talented? Just make a generalization.

Stendig: Well, I think you have various people designing chairs. You've got industrial designers doing chairs, and industrial designers qualify, or feel they qualify, to do almost any product. You've got architects doing chairs—without question, the worst. They don't know where they are. They have burned up more of their client's money by going to Tiffany people like Treitle-Gratz to make these unbelievable, unworkable chairs that don't even have to be glued together—they would never stand up. The greatest story I can tell is about Hans Corey in Switzerland, who designed a very interesting outdoor chair which won the National Award in 1939. I met him in 1957 and I asked him what he had designed since the marvelous chair of '39, and he said as he looked at me in shock, "But I won the National Award for that design. I don't design chairs anymore." Maybe that's it, once you've reached a certain stage, it's time to quit.

Question: Well, Mies designed a chair and was an architect too. I mean not all architects are——

"The versatility of integral skin urethane foam is exemplified by the range of types from soft end flexible cushioning types to impact-absorbing foams and the rigid foams suitable for structural use. Molded flexible foam applications include automotive interior trim parts such as horn buttons, arm rests and sun visors. The semirigids are used in automotive crash pads and in athletic protective gear. The rigids find application in a wide range of decorative and functional parts, everything from automotive interior trim to office desks, home furnishings, school and shop furniture."—Robert A. Stengard, "Integral Skin Urethane Foam, "*1974–1975 Modern Plastics Encyclopedia,* McGraw-Hill.

I would make the whole world out of one material if I could. . . . Anything—just one. Pancake batter!—Zographos

I am for eliminating furniture. Despite the fact that I design furniture and chairs for a living, I would like to get rid of all chairs and all furniture. I would like to just make the floor take the place of all this stuff that we think we need.—Zographos

---

Gratz: No, no, no. We've got some very good ones—Breuer, too, was an architect—but architects very often—— It gets all designers at one time or another. So they scratch something on the back of an envelope, run down to a shop, and they're either spending their money or their clients' money to have it made. Sometimes it works out well.
Zographos: But then a sociological thing prevents people from using a good office chair, even one with wheels and tilt and casters, etc., in their homes.
Question: How do you mean sociological?
Zographos: I mean what society expects you to have in your living room. It's definitely not office chairs.
Question: And what about couches? Are any of you interested in couches?
Zographos: Yes, I have done sofas and couches and sectional furniture. The same sofa or couch could be used in an office or a home.
Question: Are you in favor of couches? Do you see a couch as a single integrated material also?
Zographos: I would make the whole world out of one material if I could.
Question: What material?
Zographos: Anything—just one. Pancake batter!
Stendig: I would like to see you design the one perfect chair that you sell to everybody. Then it wouldn't have to be sold.
Question: Do you really want one chair? Would you be willing to live with only one—perfect though it may be? That's an interesting point.
Zographos: No, wait, wait. Hold it! We're not talking about one chair that will do the work of all chairs. Obviously, we're talking about a dozen different chairs to serve the dozen generalized activities that we need chairs for. It's not the same as with things like glasses and cups and plates, where we could do with one container for liquids and another for solids, period. I don't see why we have to have thousands of different glasses and shapes of dishes and sizes of this and that. They just drive us mad, these things. Or silverware, chopsticks——
Question: Well, in the nineteenth century there were a million different kinds of adjustable chairs.
Zographos: The mechanical chairs . . .
Question: They fell out of favor for some reason.
Zographos: Right.
Gratz: Well, it is generally very difficult to sell. Sales people are lazy, and that type of chair has to be demonstrated. They just do not want to take the time.
Stendig: May I add, I think customers are too lazy to alter them, or to adjust them. I mean, we have gotten complaints, "My chair is the wrong height." Why is it the wrong height? Because they didn't adjust the height mechanism. Then, "They tilt back too easily," or "——too hard." The "adjustable" chairs stay exactly the way we put them; nobody bothers to change them. They're just not popular.

Question: Last week Mr. D'Urso was talking about platforms, built-in furniture, chairs, etc. How do you feel about that in terms of future or alternate life-styles—for fun?
Zographos: Well, you are talking about a very special kind of thing now, a custom job. It can either be a custom job, or it can be a number of modular blocks that one buys to arrange in a room. I am for eliminating furniture. Despite the fact that I design furniture and chairs for a living, I would like to get rid of all chairs and all furniture. I would like to just make the floor take the place of all this stuff that we think we need.
Question: Have you ever tried living on the floor for a month?
Zographos: That's a *floor!* I don't mean *a floor!* I mean a soft floor that is raised *off* the floor.
Question: Suppose you want to eat or something like that?
Zographos: Put a tray. Actually, we do have to have some hard surfaces to work on and eat from, but I think any sitting can be done on the floor.

Moderator: Thank you all and goodnight.

Caplan (cont

In Marquand's play "The Late George Apley," one of the characters notices a book by Sigmund Freud and asks what it's about.

"Sex," he is told.

"The entire book?"

"Well, it is a bit padded."

Sex is now acknowledged as a subject with sufficient scope to justify an entire book. But chairs?

Well, why not? Like sex, chairs are both ubiquitous and misunderstood.

To design a chair for the body without knowing how the body itself is designed would be like designing an egg carton without knowing how eggs are designed. But although no package designer would commit the latter error, many chair designers commit the former. And they can get away with it. Eggs can't compensate for bad design, but chair users can and do. Since chair designers tend to have bodies, they assume they know how bodies are put together and how they work. Actually, such knowledge is hard won and there are few design awards for winning it. Niels Diffrient happened to grow up professionally in an office that emphasized human factors research, but generally I find that if a designer knows something about the body it is because, like Ward Bennett and me, he has a bad back.

In my opening talk I noted that in the vast literature of chair design relatively little attention is given to the chair as a device for supporting the human fundament. However, this was very much the subject of the seven speakers who followed me, if only—as in the case of Nicos Zographos—by indirection. Zographos candidly describes his approach as form first, function second. In any case, he contends, *sitting* is itself the cruelest design constraint, and anatomical measurements aren't all that much use to designers anyway. Carried to its logical end, Zographos's argument would hold that, for all their elegance, his chairs are no less comfortable than anyone else's chairs.

Having made his point, Zographos concentrates on *how* he goes about designing chairs. His account, Don Gratz's description of how he fabricates chairs, and Ward Bennett's

Mr. Caplan gave the last talk in the series "The Evolving Chair". (His initial lecture begins on page 8.) The above commentary was written by him as a reaction to all the lectures, including his own, as well as to the AIA Chair Design Competition presented next in this book.

observations on pitch add up to an unusually informative description of chair design process.

I can't talk about chairs for long without talking about bodies. Ward Bennett begins by discussing bodies without chairs, describing several chairless postures. These *are* functionally designed. (The lotus posture, apart from the metaphysical purpose Bennett alludes to, has the enormously practical purpose of keeping the yogi from falling on his face when he goes into a trance.)

Bennett, Mary Blade and Niels Diffrient emphasize in their talks, as too few designers do in their work, that bodies *move.* "The solution is always dynamic," Ms. Blade says. She points out that "If you drop into a chair you are suddenly loading it with at least twice your weight." The load on the chair concerns me less than the spinal compression it causes, for that force is in effect returned to the body. To *drop* into a chair is always hazardous, for it loads your spine with a weight it isn't designed to handle.

Ms. Blade calls our attention to the importance of the edge, which is truly a detail neglected at our peril. But it is not the only detail, nor is it the chief one. Edge-of-the-seat sitting is only one of the many kinds of sitting we do, and we do that kind so often only because the designed alternatives are so bad. We sit "at the edge of the seat" to watch suspense movies, because the body is poised for attack or flight. The more highly participatory a situation is, or promises to be, the closer to the edge of the seat one moves. Benched football and basketball players sit near the edge of the bench (which is backless) in the bodily expectation (however unrealistic) of being sent in, and in the excitement of watching the game.

But if sitting on the edge of a chair reflects a commitment to what is going on in front of you, it also reflects a commitment withheld from the chair. And with good reason. When the seat of a chair is too long, for example, many people can find back support only by sliding their buttocks back to the point where their feet lose contact with the floor. With the body thus cradled in the chair, the mind instantly jumps ahead to the problem of eventually getting

The fact that people don't know what's good for them does not excuse a designer from designing what *he* knows is good for them. If he knows.

out of the damned thing. We need chairs that let us sit comfortably both on their edges and deep in their interiors. We need chairs that support body language, chairs that permit expressive positions ranging from wildly enthusiastic to bored stiff.

Designers and end users need to meet each other halfway. Niels Diffrient complains that when his airline client provided instructions for using the lower-back support, passengers didn't read them, adding that they don't read instructions about how to escape from the plane in emergencies either.

Diffrient points up the difficulty of getting meaningful information. After giving a comfort test to the audience, he concludes, "Nobody knows what they're talking about." Comfort is of course subjective, and so is our response to chairs generally; but here, as elsewhere in life, there are tradeoffs. Designers, for example, are notoriously willing to suffer discomfort (or impose it on others) in return for a clean line.

In any case, it isn't so much that people don't know what they are talking about, as that people often don't know how they feel. This can lead to the classic design copout: "That's the way they want it," *they* being the consumer. The fact that people don't know what's good for them does not excuse a designer from designing what *he* knows is good for them. If he knows.

Considering the propensity of designers to talk about symbols, relatively little was said about this aspect of the chair. Yet there probably are few more powerful symbols in contemporary life. When I flashed a picture of Archie Bunker's empty chair on the screen, everyone recognized it, not just as a familiar piece of furniture, but as a collection of attitudes reminiscent of Eliot's objective correlative. That chair itself stands for a kind of good-humored bigotry. The bentwood chairs shown by Charles Stendig, the Barcelona chair, the various Eames chairs all have plainly read symbolic values. Moreover, these are real symbols, not artificially imposed status design like an arbitrary crown on a beer label or a *V* on a cigarette package.

Stemming from times when only the powerful had chairs, Chair may be the first status symbol. As such it has not held its own in American life. . . . With the advent of the modern executive suite, the chair made a comeback.

Stemming from times when only the powerful had chairs, Chair may be the first status symbol. As such it has not held its own in American life. Novelists are often our best social historians, even when they aren't our best novelists, and Sinclair Lewis was almost without parallel as a documentor of physical detail. Before he sat down to write a scene he drew elaborate maps of the immediate territory. Yet in *Babbitt,* that thoroughly modern analysis of a man's eroding self-image and values, one can hardly even find a chair. (Babbitt's power lay in his car, as Samson's resided in his hair.) With the advent of the modern executive suite, the chair made a comeback. "As long as you're up, get me a Grant's," read the Scotch ad. The speaker was not up, he was down. And what he was down in was a chair that told the reader precisely the kind of power and affluence to associate with the whiskey. The Eames lounge chair used in that campaign has been used in scores of other ads for the same reasons: it is extraordinarily photogenic and richly connotative of high status. However, power scholar Michael Korda contends that "the disposition of furniture is a better indication of power than the furniture itself."

Although D'Urso consciously designs "a room to be sat in," none of the speakers deals much with the kinds of interactions chairs permit or inhibit. The chair is rarely just an object in space; it is an object in space that may at any time have a person in it, and that is something quite different. It is, admittedly, hard to see how to factor this into design considerations, but it is just as hard to ignore such matters. I began my second Cooper-Hewitt talk by announcing that, after an opening remark or two, I would throw the session open to questions. Somehow I forgot the promise and spoke for half an hour or more, *then* asked for questions. The following exchange ensued.

Question: "That was the longest opening remark I've ever heard."
Caplan: "Yeah, you're right. I'm sorry."
Question: "Oh, I wasn't objecting."
Caplan: "Even so, why didn't you interrupt?"

The chair remains a basic component in the built environment. And since the environment will never be built once and for all, chairs will continue to get designed, made, and—if there are no better alternatives—sat in.

Over and over again, these lectures make that point: how hard it is to conceive of what a chair ought to be and to produce one that matches the concept.

Question: "Because. . . ."

Caplan: "Don't interrupt. You didn't interrupt because the room is designed so that I have the power. I'm standing above you, and you're trapped in those dreadful chairs. I would have gone on talking for another three days and you still wouldn't have found it easy to interrupt."

A designer is by definition someone who wishes for control, and a chair is a reminder of how elusive that is. "I would like to make the whole world out of one material if I could!" Zographos exclaims, making me glad he isn't God. (For that matter, I'm glad God isn't Zographos.)

The chair remains a basic component in the built environment. And since the environment will never be built once and for all, chairs will continue to get designed, made, and—if there are no better alternatives—sat in. There is in this book hardly any mention of "making statements" with chairs, although that kind of thing would have figured strongly in such talks 15 years ago. But chairs still do what they did then. (Even the novelty chairs and the rock submitted to the AIA competition are at least anti-statement statements.)

In my first talk I described the chair as a prosthetic device, a kind of stable crutch for the permanently disabled people we all are. Well, one of the more interesting of the AIA submissions *was* a prosthetic device. The jurors couldn't seem to get their minds off that submission. Apparently they couldn't get it to work very well either. In chair design, difficulty comes with the territory.

Over and over again, these lectures make that point: how *hard* it is to conceive of what a chair ought to be and to produce one that matches the concept. When some of the AIA jurors objected to a detail in a certain chair, Warren Platner reminded them that "it takes professional chair designers three years to get things like that adjusted without changing the design." In a similar exchange at the Cooper-Hewitt, Don Gratz says, "Being experienced, Nicos knows that the simplest chair base in the world will not turn out right the first time."

Being inexperienced, I didn't know that. Did you?

". . . a design credit implies that someone professionally cared, that someone—a person with a name—paid attention. That somewhere there is a real live person to be grateful to for the details that make products reliable and satisfying, and to be mad at when the things don't work."—Ralph Caplan, *Notes on Attention*, Herman Miller Inc., 1978.

Section 2

1977 The American Institute

of Architects
International
Chair Design
Competition
Submissions:

740

(All the Competition submissions are shown on the previous 18 pages to emphasize their fascinating variety. Regrettably, their creators cannot be listed due to the difficulty of completely identifying them.)

B: Cini Boeri, juror, architect and designer
E: Sherman R. Emery, juror, Editor of *Interior Design* magazine
F: Mildred Friedman, juror, Design Coordinator and Editor for *Design* Quarterly
P: Warren Platner, juror, architect and designer
C: Walter Collins, non-voting observer, Competition Director
W: Richard Saul Wurman, non-voting observer

Background: In the spring of 1976, the San Diego Chapter of the American Institute of Architects announced an International Chair Design Competition, the first of its kind since the revolutionary Museum of Modern Art furniture competitions of 1941 and 1946. Out of 502 entries submitted from around the world (the first-stage, quarter-scale models appear on the previous 18 pages), nine finalists were selected. Then the finalists were provided with $1,500 each to build full-size prototypes of their designs. The prototypes were then reviewed by the jury, and $30,000 in prize money was divided among four winning designs.

The Jury: Appointed by the AIA to judge the competition were Cini Boeri, Sherman Emery, Mildred Friedman, and Warren Platner. (Biographies on page 132.)

The Dialogue: In May of 1977, the jury met for their final deliberations. Also present were two nonvoting observers: Walter Collins, the Competition Director, and Richard Saul Wurman, who recorded the jury's informal comments (before and after the official deliberations which were sequestered) on behalf of *Chair*. (Mr. Wurman's brief biography is on page 133.) Excerpts of these comments are presented here by permission of the AIA, San Diego Chapter.

The following dialogue occurred in May of 1977 as the jury began by reviewing the nine prototypes:

B: This is nice.
E: That's very nice—Gee, is this wood? No.
F: What country was this from?
P: That was from Texas. And this is from Japan.
F: It weighs a lot. Pick it up.
P: That just makes it expensive to ship. That's all.
C: The designer said in the letter that it's not the actual material because it's too expensive to have the polycarbonate molds made.
E: So it wouldn't be that heavy in actuality?
P: Well, we don't know. It's all steel. It could be aluminum, I suppose. It doesn't seem too comfortable.
F: It hits you in the back.
E: It's nice-looking, though.
P: On these little things, I would like to point out that it takes us three years to design a chair. You gave these people one, so, just bear in mind that it takes professional chair designers three years to get things like that adjusted without changing the design. A thing like that tippiness can be adjusted.
F: Isn't it funny how you feel through the back?
P: I'm slumped forward now.
F: But sit up straight.
P: I don't want to sit up straight in this chair.
W: The seductive part is not when you're sitting in it but when it's closed.
F: That's what seduced us.

B: This is more like a toy, a play thing, than a serious chair.

P: That's what people said about Bucky Fuller's first dome: "This isn't serious—you can't really build anything that way." It's weird. I feel like a spaceman.

E: And you're supposed to carry this with you as you're going off hiking? Or walking? Wouldn't it be better just to sit on the ground?

P: Well, sit on it—for heaven's sakes. Oh, I see, it's got all kinds of adjustments.

F: Look at all the springs.

E: Amazing.

B: Wonderful—wonderful.

F: It's like sculpture—it's very beautiful.

Above is the jury, and a few of their comments while viewing the nine finalists for the first time. Beginning at the right are selected comments about the finalists which were made after the sequestered official deliberations.

Specific comments, beginning with sling chair design below:

E: I think it's designed for sustained seating—it has kept me comfortable while sitting on it. It's very compact the way it folds—it could be easily shipped. I think the proportions are a little bad—the back is too big for the seat, but that could be changed and I think it's what a chair of that kind should be.

P: It's very comfortable—spare—without any waste—forms or parts. I think it has great visual distinction. I don't know any chair that looks like that that has that character. It's comfortable in many different positions; you don't have to sit in it in any particular way. The principle of the design is complete in that it would work for a lounge chair as is shown, it would also work for an upright chair—it doesn't have arms so it isn't an ideal chair—but what chair is ideal in all respects? I think it's a very sophisticated design, very carefully worked out, and its conception is of greater distinction than anything else I've seen in this competition.

F: I agree with all those points. At the same time, I think that although it's very beautiful, it's also one of the least "new" ideas we've looked at except that it folds absolutely flat—which is a wonderful advantage. I think it needs

$10,000 Award: A folding sling-seat chair of chrome and leather. Designed by Mike Lance, San Antonio, Texas.
Lance: "I wanted the ability to take the stool apart and hang it on the wall, but preferred the sled base. I like the very pleasant sensation of being able to 'rock' back and forth, due to the lack of a rigid 'hinge' joint." Jury: "The principle of a chair that folds absolutely flat with only the thickness of the structural frame is a very sophisticated design, very carefully worked out. It is very comfortable, spare, without any waste forms or parts."

some work, minor modification in proportion and in detailing, let's say of the condition of the metal at the seat—that sort of thing. But other than that, I agree it's one of the finer entries in the competition—absolutely. It's very very pretty to look at and very comfortable to sit in.

W: Does anybody have further comment?

F: We agreed that it could be made in a smaller and upright version.

P: I think the principle of a chair that folds absolutely flat so you can pile it up with only the thickness of the structural frame——the one inch or 3/4 inch or whatever of the tubing, can be accommodated to a dining chair, a desk chair or even a sofa.

W: Do you think it's dependent on stainless steel, chrome, and leather?

F: I think the infill could be canvas or another fabric; it could even be a more interesting fabric—stitched or padded. It could be nylon net.

P: There's a universal principle here that is the important thing.

W: It's a geometry also. The folding flat is the elegance of it.

F: Yes, and that is why metal is essential—because that elegance, refinement, and smallness of detail could only be done in metal and hold up.

Folding stacking chair:

F: I'll start by saying that I think the folding mechanism is ingenious and beautiful—it's where the invention lies. I still have some hesitation about the form—I don't think it's totally resolved. When you sit in it, it still needs some work, but the folding and stacking element is beautifully done and I like it very much.

E: Its main appeal—and I hate the word—is its elegant design. It was designed by a Japanese and it's not the right proportion or scale for me or most people. It folds and stacks and is pretty to look at but is not comfortable in its present form.

P: I feel the design is complete. The dimensions are adjustable; in other words,

$10,000 Award: A stacking chair with a folding tubular chrome frame and molded plastic seat and backrest. Designed by Motomi Kawakami, Tokyo, Japan. Kawakami: "I used polyester resins with metal powder to produce the seat and back around the core. After suitable shaping, I covered them with black leather. The seat surface was made plain since the metal meshes and polyurethane gave a soft, cane-like feeling." Jury: "Again, this is quite a sophisticated design that is obviously going to work on its own terms. It is a completely finished design in principle. The folding mechanism is ingenious and beautiful, it has a distinct personality as a visual object."

there's nothing to change the appearance materially or change the principle of the structure or its structural stabilities. Therefore I feel that any criticisms of the dimensions of the chair are beside the point. I think it is a sophisticated design. It has a feature that the other chair we've just talked about does not have and that is the arms. On the other hand, I think it also has a negative feature. This chair does not fold flat and I don't know whether they will nest together. It's shown with them nesting together as folding, stacking chairs. It is less than perfect; the other chair folds completely flat and stacks completely flat. It looks to me to be a more expensive thing to produce than the other one, although I don't really know—there's no way of knowing for sure at this point.

F: The materials have not been totally worked out either. Another thing that's nice about this is that because of the position of the back, it could hang on the wall.

W: Compared to the other chair, this is minimum comfort, isn't it?

E: In its present form it is very minimum comfort!

W: But even in the proper dimensions it's still not sustained seating.

P: Less flexibility in size of person, in slouch, in how you're going to sit——

F: It relates closely to an Abbey Rents folding chair in the sense of its comfort, but in its elegance it has no relationship to that at all.

B: Particularly in the construction—extremely fine. It doesn't present something new. It's not a novelty. I would give the prize to this one mainly for the perfection with which the technical parts are made. Also, it has a very nice line.

P: It has a personality in appearance. As a visual object it has a distinct personality.

F: It's interesting that we all recognized its origin as Japanese, because there's something about the shape of that form that is like other Japanese contemporary design—— The function, the mechanism of it, and the line—and that's what we have examined so far . . .

In June of 1977 Knoll International contracted with Motomi Kawakami to explore the possibility of producing and marketing his winning design. Knoll describes this exploration process as a three- or four-month period during which they evaluate the cost, estimate the demand, describe the tooling, and look at the design as it might complement their current collection. However, at the conclusion of their exploration process, the company decided not to continue into the next, or engineering phase.

Portable convertible chair:

P: It is interesting and good because it has versatility; it folds flat—it folds to make a back rest—it folds out legs to make a chair— you can fold the backrest down and make a table out of it. I think these are interesting and useful attributes. It has a tremendous appeal as a design and it does not rely on expensive machine production methods. Anybody with a knowledge of craftsmanship could make one of these and in this day when there is such an interest in handcrafted things—this is a good example of what you can do with handcrafting to produce a really useful object. There's isn't anything about this design that I can see that is put there as decoration or decorative form or as arbitrary artwork.

E: I think he's expressed everything I feel about it—it's beautiful as an object—the craftsmanship about it. It's highly versatile and obviously highly functional.

F: Yes, I couldn't really add anything. I think the wonderful things about it, are its total flatness as it's folded up, which is something that we haven't really seen

$5,000 Award: A portable chair handcrafted of oak slats that converts to a table, a bench, or a chair. Designed by Ralph Henninger, Scottsdale, Arizona. Henninger: "The ideal situation is: no end result projected. To take a piece of wood and live with it, to get an expression of that particular piece of wood in order to put life back into it by creating a piece of furniture." Jury: ". . . it is useful in several different versions, it folds flat, it folds to make a backrest, it folds out legs to make a chair, one can fold the backrest down and make a table out of it. It is a very beautifully detailed and constructed object."

a lot of on the market. Even though this is a very special object, it requires care in the making of it, because it's wood and has dowelling. It's elegantly put together. I'm not sure this would ever be manufactured in great quantities, but I'm not sure that matters.

Adjustable strap chair:

P: I have never before been presented with the concept of a structural support that one could sit on as well as wear it as an item of clothing or accessory. This—to me anyway, is an entirely new concept—the first really new concept I've seen in seating in my life and I think it is very, very interesting. It doesn't work particularly well in detail although the highly mechanized worked-out parts of the structure that is presented obviously represent the work of someone who is thinking out this completely fresh idea. There is nothing about any of the form or any of those parts that suggest anything borrowed from any other seating objects that I've seen. I think this is a direction for the future—it's one of the few new directions that have surfaced in the world of seating, not in respect to exactly how it works but in respect to the concept of it and it could actually develop this concept into a usable item. I would like to point out that 25 years ago when Buckminster Fuller was first building his models of geodesic domes everyone was saying, Well it's a very interesting idea, very interesting structure, but how can you use it? It isn't practical. I think history shows that it took at least 10 years before that question was satisfied for most people. It might take 10 years before this design develops into something or before this concept develops into a finished design—but

$5,000 Award: An adjustable chair of aluminum with nylon webbing that is strapped to the legs and worn as a piece of clothing. Designed by Darcy Robert Bonner Jr., Dallas, Texas.
Bonner: "It is important for the 'Wearable Chair' to be adjusted to each user. Just like a piece of clothing, if the chair doesn't fit it will not feel good. When adjusted correctly you can comfortably relax with all your weight on the chair." Jury: "The concept of a structural support that one could sit on that was worn as an item of clothing is an entirely new concept—the first really new concept in seating in many years . . . the highly mechanized parts of the structure obviously represent the work of someone who is thinking out this completely fresh idea with very fresh details."

it's there—an extremely interesting concept.

B: I was about to say that I agree with Platner, but I remember that the milking stool was tied to the person.

P: I didn't know about that.

E: I hadn't thought about that.

B: It was a little wooden stool with a handle on the back, and the man approached the cow already attached to his stool, so he just had to sit down. It's as though the human body acquires an extra part.

P: That's very interesting—What you're saying is that history has shown a need for a structural support that is fastened to the person.

B: But it's not yet been really developed . . .

F: Something else is very interesting about this object. Not only is it attached to the body—I like that idea—the other thing about it is, it supports not the posterior but the back of the leg. This to me is a totally new idea. I've never seen a chair that didn't support the rump, and this does not come anywhere near the rump. It's a whole different idea about how you hold up the human body and I think that's its most important aspect.

W: It makes a triangle with your knee and your calf and your thigh, and that triangulation is the structural key.

B: The human body at the point of balance is the thigh.

F: But chairs are sat in with the rump.

E: Well, I don't quite see it as a way of the future—carrying our chairs along with us. I like it for its idea rather than what it actually is and what might be developed from it. It's a possibility, that's all.

W: Presentation is beautiful.

F: Yes, very.

P: Well, also the prototype is very beautifully made.

F: It's very well worked out and was obviously made not by hand but with access to good tools.

W: The prototype is really a testing machine for what you would really use to design the final one. It's like a furniture-machine for testing rather than the final product.

P: Since this is the most far out—most radical—with very little history to fall back on, and is not a development of something conventional which has existed for a long time, one might expect it to take longer to develop than the three years we normally require, rather than less, or the one year given.

W: The other point I made which takes it one step beyond just wearing it would be to make it a pair of pants—locking your legs into position, and you could have pants that lock.

P: As far as the visual aspects of it—I think it's a fascinating-looking device and it not only has tremendous possibilities, but it is already there. Visually, it's a handsome and intriguing—in fact, dramatically so—object, the likes of which I have never seen before.

W: And let it be said that you can't really walk with the one that has been designed. It clanks behind you.

F: It needs work.

Juror biographies:

Cini Boeri was born and educated in Milan, where she began her professional career in 1963 by opening her own studio. An accomplished architect, furniture and industrial designer, her work has been produced and exhibited internationally. Her "Suitcase on Wheels" is on permanent display at the Museum of Modern Art, and her "Gradual System" sofa model was exhibited as part of the Knoll display at the Louvre in 1972.

Sherman R. Emery was born in Maine, graduated with honors from Boston University, and received his M.A. from Columbia. As editor of *Interior Design* magazine since 1962, Mr. Emery has received several awards for outstanding journalism, including the 1966 NSID Distinguished Editorial Award and the AID Press award in 1973.

Mildred Friedman was born in Los Angeles where she received her B.A. and M.A. from the University of California. Currently acting as Design Coordinator and Editor for a number of Walker Art Center publications including *Design Quarterly,* she assisted in the design of the new Walker Art Center building in 1969 as interior designer and design consultant, and has since organized and designed installations for numerous exhibitions there.

Warren Platner was born in Ohio, studied architecture at Cornell University and now maintains an office in New Haven, Connecticut. Having successfully synthesized a wide range of design skills into a versatile practice, he is internationally known for his work in master planning, building structures, interiors, exhibitions and graphics, and designs for lighting, furniture and decoration. The recipient of numerous design awards and honors, including the Rome Prize in Architecture and the Graham Foundation Award for Advanced Studies in the Fine Arts, Mr. Platner's work has been exhibited in museums throughout the world. His wire chairs, sofas and tables were featured in the Knoll display at the Louvre in 1972.

Recording these informal comments was Richard Saul Wurman, FAIA, an architect, planner, educator, and author. Apart from his ongoing architectural practice, he is Deputy Director of OHCD in Philadelphia, Dean of the School of Environmental Design at California Polytechnical University and is the author of the *Urban Atlas* and *Notebooks and Drawings of Louis I. Kahn.*

Portable walking chair:

P: The design concept of a folding device that you carry with one hand as you might carry a cane—you can lean on it, hang it in a closet just like an umbrella or a coat hanger—has a universal appeal. It has universality of satisfaction of a need that you don't get in most other kinds of furniture.

Obviously the idea of something you strap onto your legs and wear as a piece of clothing has limited usefulness. I think this is a little less interesting and radical, it nevertheless has a certain uniqueness to it in that it has a back support—it has a complete seat, you're not just sitting on a couple of points—it has a tripod leg arrangement which could be stable if the folding mechanism was properly made. And as I said before, the thing is very light.

It is imperfect and doesn't work completely as far as stability goes in the prototype that we have here, but I feel without any question that that could be solved. I think it has minimal seating comfort—it's better than a racetrack cane—it's better than sitting on a fireplug. You can carry it with you, it can stand up by itself—so that if you want to leave it in its sitting position, you can stand up and then sit down again without looking for it. It will stay there. All the other devices I know like this such as a racetrack cane will not.

Finalist: A portable walking chair of aluminum tubing and molded plastic. Designed by Gregory John Cook, Houston, Texas.
Cook: "The Walking Chair is designed for mobility. Closed for transport, this lightweight unit provides assistance in walking and, with weight concentrated about the handle, swings smoothly and quickly in response to one's gait." Jury: "Very portable."

B: I don't think it is too good-looking—I think it's ugly. Functionally, it takes from other models of things that rest the body. And as for the mechanism, it really doesn't function, and won't, even if there are two more years of work put into it. The concept that has three legs that have to be opened like an umbrella will not give complete success. Also, the form is not well studied—and the angle and the seat—— This design doesn't have much hope or much future.

E: I'm afraid I don't really like it very much. I don't think that if it were developed so that it did work—stabilized—that anyone would carry it say to the ball game, racetracks, or anywhere. Even though it's very light, I find it to be too awkward to slip over my arm like an umbrella.

F: I guess what I liked about it is not the idea (which the camp stool might serve better) but simply the way it looks. It's an amusing object. I like it the way I like a sports car—you know, not because it's a better car but because I like the way it looks.

P: I'd like to meet the originator, the man who developed this, because I think it can be developed. I would like to see it proceed into a developed, completed thing, because I think it will succeed.

F: Right. And there's something else I would like to propose and I don't know if this should be on the tape, but it occurs to me that maybe we are giving a lot of attention to ideas that aren't very interesting and maybe we should be giving more attention to the ideas that are more interesting but less well developed. In other words, we are being terribly conservative in our allocation of money and attention.

P: I understand what you are saying. The only thing is, this is a chair design competition—and there's a certain limitation with what you can do with chairs and the fact that for centuries they have developed in a certain direction. There are reasons why they have developed that way and I don't think those will change. I do think the horizons of what a chair can be will expand and we have here at least one idea that potentially expands that horizon but I don't think that in a competition like this you're only looking for a far-out idea that pushes horizons. I think you're also looking for concepts within the conventional framework of what we and civilization consider a chair to be. Working within that framework—a fresh conception in some manner, an object that is using all the conventional restrictions, still has a unique character of its own and a personality of its own. Those two designs, which you would call "conventional," have that. I think you would agree that they have that.

B: The conventional form can be surpassed only by a better usage of the chair—otherwise, a chair must be a chair—and must function as a chair.

"The contact proofs (of all the submissions) are an historic document, a collection of wonderful and weird, chairs with humor and some with tumors, rocks and reproductions of what, alas, somebody else had done long ago and better. The models are extraordinary, beautifully made at one-quarter scale. The quality of these models, as shown in the contact proofs, are of particular consistency."—Wurman

"Purposes: To encourage the development of original designs by the award of prize money. To help to fruition the design in that they may be manufactured and sold."—Chair Competition Program.

"Definition of CHAIR as it relates to this competition: 'Any device which can support the human body in a sitting position.'"—Supplementary Competition Information Sheet, September 1976.

Rump-rest chair:

W: Is there any comment anyone wants to give on the workers' rump-rest posture?

B: If you told me that this has already been on the market made in exactly the same way, then I would agree to eliminate it. Otherwise, I think we should take it into consideration.

E: Even if it weren't on the market, the idea's very good. But I find it to be a very awkward way to achieve what it was meant to.

Finalist: A "Worker's Rump-Rest Posture Chair." Designed by Societadi Ergonamia Applicata (Luigi Bandini Buti, Gabriel Cortili, Enrico Moretti, Cajo Punio Odescalchi, Isaco Hosoe, and Pietro Salmoiraghi), Milan, Italy.
Designers: "The 'Worker's Rump-Rest Posture Chair' has a seat which is adjustable to the environment to assure easy motion and safety for the workers and others. This chair's characteristics should vary in accordance with the worker's need of motion."

P: My feeling about this is that it is more like a piece of factory equipment. It is not a chair. The folding cane, the strap-on things are things that any person could use universally around the world in different situations. This is a very, very specific piece of equipment needed to do a very, very specific, limited task. It seems to me that it isn't worthy of an award simply because it has such limited usefulness.

E: I agree.

F: There are a lot of construction lines that have similar devices built into them as part of the equipment—you know, where the person can lean back or rest briefly. I'm sure this exists in one form or another.

P: It is similar in some respects to the special seating that we developed in the public observation deck on top of the World Trade Center, in that it only meets certain specialized needs in certain specialized conditions. I don't think it should be classified as a chair. I guess I do not believe that you can divorce the tractor seat from the tractor and give it a prize.

(Below left) Finalist: A chair cut from a single sheet of plywood that folds flat for storage. Designed by Masazo Tano, Milan, Italy.
Jury: "Good economy with one piece of plywood. Good portability."

(Middle) Finalist: A stacking chair of steel tubing and fiberglass. Designed by Innenarchitekten (Annette Stahl-Baumeister and Guido Berger), Basel, Switzerland. Designers: "The idea was developed to satisfy the special requirements of a chair for public use out of doors, e.g., in garden restaurants, parks, and private gardens. With single seat lamellae placed next to one another and the appropriate frame, particularly stable stacking chairs, arm chairs and benches could be constructed." Jury: "Good flexibility."

B: The other two are also not chairs—they are either a piece of the human body or a stick.

P: This is part of the tractor.

B: And the other one is part of your body.

P: But anybody can use that—you don't have to be a worker.

B: This is the only one that works—it has a specialized use.

P: Well, okay, but I see it as a piece of factory equipment rather than a chair.

B: You didn't specify in the competition that there would be a chair for the home only—that one for the street—that one for the stadium or any kind of place—and this one for the factory.

E: You don't even fit in there—you're not in a sitting position when using it. I think in a chair you have to get in a sitting position.

(Right) Finalist: Molded plastic chair using a single modular element for its back seat and legs. Designed by Centro Progettazione (Massimo Fusco, Robert Gangemi, Marco Cianfanelli, Simberto Senni Buratti, and Rinaldo Stralanchi), Firenze, Italy. Designers: "The proposed system is based on the use of only one basic element which gives rise to a wide range of possible sittings by means of several assembling methods. Jury: "Prototype not functional. However, the design could easily be produced. Practical modular elements."

P: It's like a fence rail—you can sit on a rail. It's an adjustable rail.

C: I've come up with a definition that says this was for any device that supports the human body.

F: Then we could have entries that were essentially beds——

Additional three finalists (above):

P: The concept of what a chair is is probably the most interesting aspect of this competition. I think, in the sense of what we have selected as winners, perhaps less interesting than the range of concepts that have been represented by what people have sent in. Some people have clearly conceived of a chair as an amusing toy and nothing else. Some people have

Competition Committee: Walter Collins (Director), Douglas Austin, A.I.A., Marshall Brown, Marti Bundy, San Diego A.I.A., Richard Bundy, A.I.A., Pat Cobb, Linda Kaczur, Jack L. Mahan, Jr., Ph.D., Russell Rex. Sponsors: The San Diego Chapter, AIA, Fine Arts Gallery of San Diego, The Graham Foundation, Fortress Furniture Company, General Fireproofing, Knoll International, Steelcase Furniture Company.

sent in stuffed animals made of fabric and stuffing as examples of chair design. One person sent in a stone—just a rock out of nature. Obviously that is a valid concept of a chair. You can go out and find it—it's a found object that functions as a chair.

Some people have considered chairs as simply a piece of sculpture. We had many submissions that are obviously that—they wouldn't be very comfortable to sit in. They are big deals as far as visual construction; they have extraneous forms that have nothing to do with seating comfort; they have nothing to do with supporting the human body; they are just sculptural manifestations of form and material—— That's a conception of what a chair can be—a sculptural object. Other people have thought in terms of strictly the human body and the minimum support. We had one thing that was sent in which was nothing but a flat sling like a hammock and you just lay in it. In fact, it was very well presented because the person lying in it was nude and it suggested the human body in a very forceful way.

Oh yes, we had a piece of clothing sent in as a chair. It was a cape that you could wear and was lined with a waterproof vinyl material or something like that and if you wanted to sit down as we're sitting down on wet ground here, you simply sat down on the cape which was a piece of clothing. It was not a device you fastened to your body to support yourself like those leg supports that we have decided to cite with an award, but it is a different concept—just a piece of clothing that could be construed as a chair.

E: There were some very handsome models, but most of them were derivative or really have been done before—lacking in originality. Some of them would make very good chairs if they were executed to full models, but they're really variations on old themes.

P: I wanted to elaborate on something that Sherman said. This would be a very disappointing competition indeed if you considered it only in respect to design for chairs that you could put right into production and which would sell well in a department store or furniture showroom. There were not very many designs, only two really, that we have thought were worthy of that, plus having distinction in other ways. There have been many, many variances on chair designs with distinctive personalities that have been submitted. That is

"The comments are presented here in the pure and unpolished reality of conversation. For me, the re-experiencing of the jury's comments in print is a rare insight into the competition process."—Wurman

All photographs in this section were taken by Sandra Williams, of Robert Ward/Sandra Williams, Photography of Architecture, San Diego, California.

inherent in enterprises of this kind. If you're going to get 600 entries, you're going to have a lot that are variations and copies of things that already exist.

And another category of entry. We had many caricatures and cartoons of chairs where the person thought of a chair as being an exaggerated parody on an existing object or existing design. We had another category in which people thought of chair design as being a reconstruction of historical design. Somebody submitted a very beautiful model in a glass case—which was not as nice as Reitveld's design—and several other reincarnations of famous designs. Obviously these are not fresh ideas and neither are they fresh designs.

F: Several of my favorites fall into that category. The wonderful teddy bear. I'm looking for Queen Elizabeth and I can't find her——

E: That's a chair for only the Queen to sit on. It's a Jubilee chair—when she sits on it, it plays "God Save the Queen" and everyone stands up.

F: There were any number of handsome chairs that could go into production tomorrow; we didn't select them because there was no originality present.

F: And I think it is very important to make that point. Not that they were poor, but simply that there was nothing interesting about them.

W: I was very impressed when I got the contact sheets with the variations on the theme and the general level of excellence of the models—the care, the sensibility, the fun and the humor of the responses.

P: And the historical styles . . .

F: Chippendale . . . In a way they were taunting the jury, which was fine.

E: I remember there was one thing you liked, Warren. Stacking chairs in rattan.

P: I was interested in those—that it was a method of design and construction of a chair that most of the world could achieve without industrialization.

E: And it probably would sell.

P: But we decided it wasn't a fresh-enough design.

P: Here's the rock. That's it. It was from Italy.

W: Was it actually a stone?

P: Yes. It was a quarter-scale model of a stone. I wanted to select it so they would be required to send the full-size one in. The jury wouldn't agree with me.